Elements of Performance

Choreography and Dance Studies

A series of books edited by Muriel Topaz and Robert P. Cohan, CBE

Please see the back of this book for other titles in the Choreography and Dance Studies series.

Elements of Performance

A Guide for Performers in Dance, Theatre and Opera

Pauline Koner

The Juilliard School of Dance, New York, USA

ho ap

harwood academic publishers
Australia ● Canada ● China ● France ● Germany ● India
Japan ● Luxembourg ● Malaysia ● The Netherlands
Russia ● Singapore ● Switzerland

First published 1993
Second printing 1998

Amsteldijk 166
Ist Floor
1079 LH Amsterdam
The Netherlands

Front cover photo: the author, Improvisation, Leningrad 1936, photographer unknown.
Back cover photo: the author, photographer Herbert Migdol.

Excerpts:

Reprinted from *Centering in Pottery, Poetry and the Person* c. 1989 by Mary Caroline Richards, Wesleyan University Press, by permission of University Press of New England.

The Language of Dance by Mary Wigman/Walter Sorell (1966), Wesleyan University Press, by permission of University Press of New England.

Song of the Lark by Willa Cather (1915). Familiar Quotations by John Bartlett (1955).

What is Art? by Count Leo Tolstoy (1898). Familiar Quotations by John Bartlett (1955).

Art by Ralph Waldo Emerson, Black's Readers Service.

Library of Congress Cataloging-in-Publication Data

Koner, Pauline.
   Elements of performance: a guide for performers in dance,
theatre, and opera / by Pauline Koner.
      p. cm. – – (Choreography and dance studies; v. 3)
   Based on the course of the same title the author teaches at the
Juilliard School of Dance.
   Includes index.
   ISBN 3–7186–5266–8 (softcover)   ISBN 3–7186–5309–5 (hardcover)
   1. Dancing – – Study and teaching.   2. Movement (Acting) – – Study and
teaching.   I. Title. II. Series.
GV1589.K66 1993
792.8'07 – – dc20

                              93–6042
                                CIP

For All My Students

Past — Present — and Future

Contents

Introduction to the Series

Choreography and Dance Studies is a book series of special interest to dancers, dance teachers and choreographers. Focusing on dance composition, its techniques and training, the series will also cover the relationship of choreography to other components of dance performance such as music, lighting and the training of dancers.

In addition, *Choreography and Dance Studies* will seek to publish new works and provide translations of works not previously published in English, as well as publish reprints of currently unavailable books of outstanding value to the dance community.

Robert P. Cohan

PREFACE

I was perplexed. I had a gnawing sensation that something very vital was missing, but could not pin it down. It was 1956, while I was teaching at the American Dance Festival, Connecticut College, New London, Connecticut. There were excellent technique and choreography classes, with enthusiastic students working day and night to get the most from this summer session. They could move beautifully. They could choreograph - what was bothering me? Then it dawned on me: many of the students had no inkling of how to perform. They looked wonderful in the studio, but their performance fell flat when they were on stage. I suddenly realized that knowing how to perform is a very special art.

I was an instinctive performer. It all came naturally. In order to know consciously what I did, I would have to dig and analyze the what and the how. I would have to formulate a theory and a method in order to teach this demanding art. I decided to name the course The Elements of Performance. I would not worry about the physical technique but would concentrate on those qualities that use that technique for the ultimate goal: to perform as an artist. I consulted with Doris Humphrey, explaining what I had in mind and expressing my interest in introducing this unique course the following year. She responded enthusiastically: "Pauline that is a terrific idea and you are the one to do it."

There were a few books on acting (Stanislavski's An Actor Prepares and The Making of a Character) that had given me some ideas of how I might approach the subject. Basically, I would have to search within myself and watch others like José Limón, Martha Graham, Charles Weidman, and other performers to capture the essence of performing.

In 1957 I initiated the course at the American Dance Festival and have been teaching and developing it ever since. The subject matter became clearer and kept growing as I challenged myself more. I learned from watching my students grow. Their change was so obvious that I knew I was working in the right direction. Furthermore, I discovered that many of the principles applied to all of the performing arts.

Actors, opera singers and even musicians can benefit from inner focus, muscle intensity, rhythmic timing, breathing - essentials for any performance. Beyond that, there is always the need to have a concept of a work as a whole so that the development and contrast have impact. When musicians use the interval between movements as a rest rather than a transition, the flow of the composition is fragmented. A true artist will never allow this to happen. It is most important to maintain concentration, even if a string needs replacing or a brow needs wiping. The silence is a transition from one mood to another, and that transition is vital to the whole. Dancers, actors, and singers must use tacit moments on stage by creating an inner activity, moving in time if not in space. This keeps the performance alive. Inner focus - total concentration every moment one is on stage - is the key to keeping both the performer and the viewer involved.

I trust that this book may offer provocative and constructive ideas that may be of interest to all performers.

Note on Diagrams

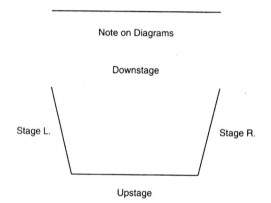

Downstage

Stage L.   Stage R.

Upstage

Acknowledgments

Writing this book presented a challenge, for I had to translate inner qualities as well as movement into words.

I am grateful to Barbara Palfy for her discerning editing.
I am grateful to Arno Jacobson for his sensitive line drawings.
I am grateful to Muriel Topaz for suggesting the publishers.
I am grateful to Evelyn Shepard for her help these many years.
I am grateful to my friend Kay Turney for her moral support.

WHAT IS PERFORMANCE ?

To perform is to perform is to perform, is

to exhibit or illumine, is

To Do or To Be

A performance is a performance is a performance

A performance can be an exhibition of self

A performance can be a technical display

A performance can be a revelation

To Be

involves a search - a transformation from outer self to inner self, from performer as acrobat to performer as artist. It is said one is born with it: that very electric quality that spellbinds the audience - grasps its attention - leaves an unforgettable impression. We call it presence.

I believe that every performer has a seed that needs nurturing. In some this seed will develop faster and better than in others. But the seed will take root, will grow, and may blossom if one is a seeker, a challenger, a questioner. M.C. Richards says in Centering in Pottery, Poetry, and the Person "We are transformed not by adopting attitudes toward ourselves but by bringing into center all the elements of our sensations and our thinking and our emotions and our will: all the realities of our bodies and our souls. All the dark void in our undiscovered selves."

We must ask "Who am I? What am I doing on this stage? Why am I doing this? How can I find the essence?" As a brilliant technician one may thrill the audience. As an artist one will move the audience. Communication! That is what it is all about. A mood, an impression, an idea from the deepest core of being to the deepest core of being. Communication from a source that is constantly growing, changing, evolving.

For the growing, the study of technique is essential, but from the very beginning we must never lose sight of the spirit. The technique must not overshadow that living breathing force - the center of our being. Again to quote Richards, "An act of self from me to you from center to center. We must mean what we say from our innermost heart to the outermost galaxy . . . We carry light within us. There is no need to reflect. Others carry light within them. These lights must wake to each other."

After many years I am still searching for essentials; there always seems to be more to discover. My primary interest is not in technical ability - it is either there already or will be acquired - but in transcending the mechanics and finding the spirit of the movement. At present there is too much technique and not enough of the person on stage. A performance should never be an ego trip. Once you have discovered why you are performing you will work differently, since your concept comes from within.

Many dancers are inhibited or shy. By immersing themselves in the doing, the being, they can shed the externals. I call it peeling the banana skin and getting to the you - the real you. I do not want any two people to be alike. You are all different. Each of you has a unique personality. I care much about that difference, about you the person, the individual. Individuality is important; it should be developed rather than subdued. But that individuality must also be subject to the discipline of the choreographer or director of a particular performance.

The Elements of Performance course is divided into two components. The Primary Elements deal with the art - emotion, motivation, focus, dynamics, and movement texture, which are as vital as fire, air, earth, and water are to life. The Secondary Elements deal with the craft, and include an analysis and study of stage levels - platforms, steps, boxes, and ladders; hand props - fans, Chinese ribbons, elastic, hoops, chairs; fabric - various lengths and textures of cloth; costumes - long skirts, caftans, and period suggestions; finally stage decorum - bows, entrances and exits, and general precautions.

As the elements of the art and the craft are learned and absorbed they become part of your being. Although each element is taken separately and absorbed mentally you must remember that they are part of a unified whole. That mental understanding must be transformed into a kinesthetic feel, an emotional and body reflex that transcends thought. You are illumined within. When that happens, a performance becomes a revelation both for the performer on the stage and the viewer in the audience.

In the text I discuss the underlying principles of all the various elements and give methods for doing the exercises in class or on your own. Some of the exercises are structured, but many are improvisations. Improvising in a classroom helps performance immensely. You become involved with what you are doing and lose the fear and inhibitions that overtake you on stage. You are not self conscious or thinking about press criticism. This total involvement transfers to the stage and gives you belief in what you are doing. You must maintain that sense of total involvement on stage to be an artist.

The text is addressed to the performer (with occasional asides to the instructor). For expediency, I use certain abbreviations and expressions throughout:

R - right: L - left:

Improv - improvisation

Rhythm is given in dancers' counts, as steps, or spelled out:

A single number = quarter note

& = eighth note

1& = two eighths notes

1&a = two sixteenths and one eighth note

Stagger - consecutive entrances when there is more than one.

Spiral - rotate wrist from side to side making a figure 8.

I
PRIMARY ELEMENTS
THE ART

PART 1 - FOCUS

Emotion and motivation need little explanation. As living beings we all feel emotion of some sort. Motivation, as well, is an absolute. It exists in everything we do. In performing, just feeling good or pride in the doing can be a motivation. To decide not to want motivation is in itself a motivation. Without a motivation of some sort we would be zombies, unless of course we were motivated to play the role of a zombie.

We do not even realize how often and in how many ways we use the word "focus." The focus of your eyes - the focus of an idea - the focus of a campaign - the focus of a camera - the focus of a painting - the focus of a choreographic work - the focus of a parade and on and on. Yet in performance if someone says, "They are not focusing properly" it usually means they are not looking where expected. But this is only one aspect of the totality of focus.

Focus is to the mind what gravity is to the body - a basic force. I like to think of it as a many faceted jewel. Each facet is a specific kind of focus. Just as a jewel reflects various colors, so do the various kinds of focus depending on the specific need. The dictionary definition is:

1 - A center of awareness.

2 - A point of concentration.

3 - A concentration of attention.

4 - A center of activity, attraction, or attention.

What are the words that are repeated, that seem important?

Center, which is the core of focus.

Concentration, which is the essence of focus.

I have divided focus into six categories: Inner, Directional, Area, Magnetic, Body, and Dramatic. Although it is important to fragment this jewel by exploring each facet separately, eventually they are all integrated into our thinking and our feeling. At least two of the above are essential at all times, since inner focus is always necessary and any one or more of the others may be required by the motivation. The important thing to remember is that all of the above are basically the one element - FOCUS. Although inner focus is primary, I find it easier for teaching purposes to start with a more obvious facet.

DIRECTIONAL FOCUS

This involves points of attention. It demands a concentration of eyes and mind on a specific still point in a specific direction: forward, back, up, down, sideways - and a moving point in any direction. It also involves varying gradations and combinations of these directions. For instance you can be focusing forward and moving forward with eyes either diagonally down, at eye level, or diagonally up.

Many dancers, when travelling in space, are so involved with their body movement that they do not know why they are going in that direction. The motivation might be design, the meeting of a partner, or a dramatic demand to be at a certain place, whatever it is there is the need to get there. That need must show in the eyes and in the body.

Do not stare but look, not only look but see! The difference in these three words is tremendous. Staring may be an absence of looking and looking is not necessarily seeing. Seeing is looking at a point, object, or person and registering consciously what is seen. The eyes and the mind are totally in harmony. However, staring can be used to express a trance, insanity, being in a vacuum, or so intensely involved with an inner thought that seeing is not desired.

Directional focus is of utmost importance in relation to the use of space. You become aware of the space, rather than just aware of the body.

1 - Travelling Forward

I ask for a simple walking base and usually find it a problem. Few dancers know how to walk beautifully - body buoyant, controlled, travelling effortlessly, smoothly through space, sailing through space. Instead one is apt to see slouching, shoulder wagging, arms wiggling, or a walk where the back leg passes through while the weight remains on the standing leg. Try running to catch a bus with the latter movement and see what happens. With the foot leading the body, forget catching that bus. Walking is one of the most difficult movements because it is so simple, so open, so revealing. Let us try what we normally do in life. We need to get somewhere. What do we do? We lead with the upper part of the body, not the feet. Our weight is shifted to the foot stepping forward leaving the other foot behind. The body leads - you, the person, want to get there. However it is most important to stylize this walk, for as a dancer the entire body must be under control: no slouching, no shoulder wagging, arms hanging but holding the air - we must use the balls of the feet, articulate the instep, glide, travel lightly, take over the space: I call this a functional walk.

There are two kinds of walk: the <u>Functional Walk</u> and the <u>Ceremonial Walk</u>. Most dancers are accustomed to the second and when asked to travel in space on a walking base will most likely respond with the latter. The dancer steps forward and pulls the back foot forward with a very pointed toe and bent knee so that the foot leads the body. There is no urgency or need to get somewhere. The body is placed from spot to spot and cannot travel quickly. This is excellent when used for ceremony, but it is vital for the dancer to learn the functional walk for use in Directional Focus so that they can move at any speed.

A second problem I encounter is that of keeping an exact beat no matter how simple the rhythm. Very often dancers tend to rush the double beat (1&). They are so accustomed to complicated movement that a simple walk seems too easy, therefore there is an inclination to rush. Furthermore it is necessary to remember the importance of concentrating on a specific point without wavering or shifting.

Method
Rhythm 1 2 3& 4

Pick a point and travel toward that point with the above rhythm or any other rhythm you wish. Mean to go there! Establish the sense of need to get to that point.

Step R 1, L 2, R L 3&, R 4.

Continue across floor - alternating feet at 1 of each new phrase.

Shifting direction forward

Rhythm: 1 2 3 4& 5& 6 - 1 (2) 3 4 5 6

Pattern moves from stage L to stage R on walking base

R 1 - L 2 - R 3

step front L 4 - together R &,

back L 5 - together R & - front L 6

(front together back together front - 4& 5& 6)

step upstage R 1 - hold 2 - step L 3, one half turn right

walk down stage R 4 - L 5 - R 6.

Continue walking forward facing stage right

starting with L 1 - R 2 - L 3

step front R 4 - together L & -

back R 5 - together L & - front R 6

(front together, back together, front -4& 5& 6)

face down stage L 1 - hold 2 - step R 3, one half turn left

walk upstage L 4 - R 5 - L 6

Repeat pattern toward stage left.

Counts for the three parallel arrows: __ 4& __ 5& __ 6

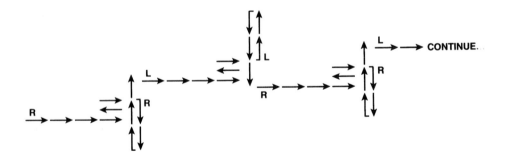

Variation forward

Rhythm: 1 2& 3 4&

Zig-zag pattern direction forward from upstage left to stage right Start with the R foot travel downstage diagonal right.

R 1 - L R 2& - L 3 - R 4&

turn head sharply left on & beat of 4. Start with L foot repeat pattern downstage diagonal left.

The head must always turn sharply to the new direction. Keep repeating the phrase.

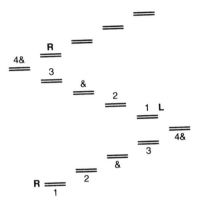

This exercise can be done solo or in twos. Stagger entrance every two bars and then every bar. I often ask those waiting to shout or make some kind of sound on the count of 4. This motivates the change of head and new direction on the & beat.

2 - Travelling Forward Focusing Back

Rhythm: legato 1 2 3 4 5

Step on L foot and raise R leg attitude back, as head turns back. With eyes focusing back, raise both arms extended as though lifting a veil in front of the face 1 2 3 4

Step forward on R foot while lowering arms and head and turning body forward 5

Keep repeating travelling stage R

Stagger in two bars.

Repeat on the opposite leg travelling from stage R to stage L. This movement takes on an archaic look and with rhythmic variations becomes an interesting dance phrase.

Comment:

Travelling forward and focusing forward implies going toward. Travelling forward and focusing back implies going from. Travelling back and focusing back implies going toward.

Travelling back and focusing forward implies going from.

The use of directional focus alone can introduce a dramatic idea.

3 - Focusing Up and Down

Generally there is a tendency to look up with the head at only a slight tilt. To really look up and see the head must bend back enough so that the eyes look directly up. To watch a bird swooping in the sky the entire plane of the face will be directed upward. There are three joints at the top of the spine that allow for tilting the head without collapsing the neck. It is important to stretch the back of the neck when looking up.

Initially when asked to look down, most dancers will hinge forward at the hips. To look at your toe this can seem quite silly. If a caterpillar creeps across your foot, what happens to your body? The back curves down in a rounded shape, the eyes look down to discover what is there. Use the real-life gesture and stylize it. Be so involved that it shapes your body, the entire stretching up or curving down. The body signals the seeing.

Involvement is an absolute. It is a primary factor in all performance, be it by dancers, actors, singers, or musicians. If performers keep involved, if they believe deeply in what is happening, whether moving or in stillness, the audience cares. Observe someone in the street looking up intently at something in the sky and then one, two, and soon a crowd will be looking up. They are curious; they are involved. What do they see up there? It may actually be nothing, but the involvement of the initial person has forced the response.

Method

Rhythm: 1 2& 3 4 or any simple rhythm

Walk across the floor looking up: follow a bird; reach up with the spine and tilt the head back; see that bird with the whole body.

1 2& 3 4.

Look down: see a caterpillar; let the spine curve and really see that caterpillar. 1 2& 3 4 (alternate the phrase).

Stagger in two bars.

4 - Combine all Four Directions: forward, back, up, down.

Rhythm 1 2& 3 in a staircase pattern.

Start upstage L to stage R on right foot focus forward 1 2& 3

One quarter turn L travel down stage focus back 1 2& 3

One quarter turn R travel stage R focus up 1 2& 3

One quarter turn L travel down stage focus down 1 2& 3

Repeat: opposite side starting with L foot. Stagger in two bars

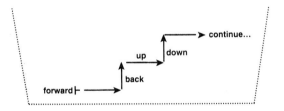

(Since the pattern with the change of direction may be confusing, it is wise to start by allowing the entire group to walk the pattern in unison.) The directional changes should be sharp with a slight attack, the arms held buoyant at the sides of the body.   Then stagger in one bar. This creates an exciting counterpoint.

The full use of the head is of utmost importance.

5 - Central Point

Rhythm: 1 2&a 3 4&

Choose a center point on floor. Moving in a large circle, never take the eyes from that point. Stagger in one bar. Suppose this is a magic ritual - to look away is to die. Move in the circle sideways, facing the center, eyes cast obliquely down toward the point. The angle of the eye is important. Be hypnotized by that point. The central point need not be on the floor; it can be anywhere in space from the floor to the ceiling.

6 - Moving Point

Method

Standing in one place, follow with the eyes a person slowly walking past in front from stage L to stage R and back again. This is no problem. Now, imagine that person walking past. The mind and the eye must concentrate and see the imaginary figure moving in the same path. The entire body must be involved although not moving in space. One can give the impression of seeing various activities simply by the speed with which the eyes and head move. (i.e.- a tennis match or a car racing by).

Comment:

A point can move in any direction: down to up, up to down, in a circle in front of the body or in a circle around the body with the eyes following and the body turning when absolutely necessary.

7 - Improvs

Central and multi-directional

Rhythm: 1 2 3 4 5 6 (Slow tempo for three to six people).

Set a fixed point in space. Change the direction of movement in space on each count of 1 without ever taking the eyes from the focal point. Freeze the position after the sixth bar. Improv should be dance movement using space.

Reverse the problem. On each count of 1 change directional focus making the shifts extreme.

Comment:

A central point unifies the group.

A shifting point fragments the group (this can be very useful in choreography).

Various kinds of directional focus;

These should be solo improvisations. Make the viewers recognize the differences. It is interesting to be given a specific technical dance phrase, involving two or more kinds of directional focus.

I have found it is much easier to think of the rhythmic patterns in terms of sounds, rather than numbers. Sound and movement are the only two art forms that are organic. The body is that wonderful instrument that makes them come alive. Nothing comes between the doing and the receiving. In dancing, it helps sometimes to fulfill a movement by actually making an audible sound during the learning process as well as for an added effect in performance.

Comment:

Directional focus intensity is the concentration of the visual and emotional intensities for both the performer and the viewer.

1 - In order to be oblivious of the audience you must be totally involved with what is happening on stage.

2 - A point of attention should never be directly at the audience except for comedy or for a specific dramatic reason.

3 - The eye of the performer which looks at and sees a person, object, or an imaginary image, attracts the attention of the viewer.

4 - Staring, except when motivated, causes the viewer to wander.
(i.e. - being in a vacuum, blindness, insanity, shock or seeing nothing)

5 - Do not diffuse! Concentrate!

6 - Continuity of focus is an essential!

7 - The word <u>involved</u> is the key to any true performance.

8 - In all improvs do not only think of the particular problem but consider it a performance. The endings should always be held till all the vibrations have ceased. Never forget that beginnings and endings frame what you do. If the intensity is dropped too soon, a lovely moment can be ruined.

AREA FOCUS

Dimensions

For the dancer space is alive
It pulsates
Its proportions shift
So do its shapes.
Space must be grasped
  molded, embraced.

The life force of the body,
  its electricity,
The life force of dance,
  its mobility,
Changes space.
As the dancer ventures
  within it,
Space vibrates.
The life force of space
Changes dance.

Space is infinite - space is boundless - it surrounds us totally.

We must take this external void and define it for our particular needs.

Area focus involves areas of awareness: a concentration of mind and eyes to encompass a specific area. It is a concept dictated by motivation that internalizes the size of the performer's space rather than accepting the given space (studio or stage) as an absolute. That given space can be transformed by the performer from the smallest space to the whole outdoors. That power of transformation happens by virtue of concentration on an inner belief. The given space is altered, it disappears.

For the sake of experiment I have arbitrarily created five areas of awareness, although there may be many gradations between each area. The area of solitude is a feeling of utter aloneness, of being apart, a sense of complete isolation. It is important to explore the inner feelings about the space around you. It is a very small space that separates you from the rest of the world. Although you may be in a very large space, this small area of your conscious being moves with you wherever you may be on the stage. An awareness of the area of the stage is perhaps the most difficult to achieve. You must

15

convey the sense of that space with nothing beyond it; enclosed on four sides. You must create the fourth wall between you and the audience. As the area expands to the auditorium there is no fourth wall. The space has opened up to include the auditorium but not the audience, for you are dealing just with the awareness of space. The area of the horizon gives a sense of great distance, of seeing beyond the walls to the very horizon in any direction, while that of the sky or open space gives a sense of being out-of-doors. All the boundaries of the stage totally disappear. There are no walls.

Method

In working with these areas I use a single ground base 1 2 3 & 4 5 which is constant. The entire pattern is done facing front.

Step to the R with R foot - 1

step upstage with L foot - 2

step to L two steps R L - 3 &

Step downstage R L - 4 5

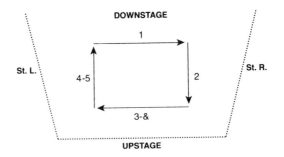

This is done four times to the R. Take a catch-step to reverse direction. Repeat four times to the L. Finish with an extra step forward and hold. (In teaching this, it is helpful to have the entire group work together till they have mastered the pattern on both sides.)

1 - Area of Solitude

Look into yourself. Find the inner image of feeling isolated. The space is small, as if you are enclosed in a tube. It is wise in the beginning to cast the eyes down. A downcast eye helps to isolate yourself and limit the surroundings. After mastering this inner quality, the eyes may be at any angle as long as you can maintain the feeling of aloneness. The viewer must feel that aloneness, the complete isolation. Never forget that you are dancers, the body is always in control. It must always be alive, even though you may be doing very little. This does not imply body tension but rather an intensity that controls the entire body. Breathing properly is an essential and as our consciousness of the areas increases, the increase of breath plays an important role.

2 - Area of the Stage

The awareness of enlarging the area is helped by the level of the eyes, obliquely down at first, giving the impression of an enclosed space. However you should not depend on the angle of the eyes. The increase of breath changes the sense of the body. As you breath more deeply the body expands more. It feels larger and the eyes now encompass the stage as a whole.

3 - Area of the Auditorium

The front wall is gone. You do not see the audience as solitary individuals but feel them as a collective whole. You see greater space. The eye level is higher, the breathing deeper. At first, these changes may be difficult. It takes time to achieve a sense of the difference in space. Eventually you will find a way to adjust and really feel and believe that this is the particular area you need for a particular idea. The gradation of the difference in this instance is more extreme, than that of the first two areas.

4 - Area of the Horizon

Try to see a tremendous distance, where the earth meets the sky. See through the walls of the theater. With the eyes focused obliquely up, imagine seeing something very far away. This area involves the change from indoor to outdoor awareness. Somehow it seems easier to achieve than the previous changes which are more subtle - more demanding, in the difference of the sense of space.

5 - <u>Area of the Sky</u>

Now, open the space, break open the walls, the ceiling. You might be somewhere in an open field and sky above. The outdoors is your space, totally, completely. The breathing is deeper, the body expands even more, and you may want to raise your arms higher to encompass the space. The space surrounds you rather than your seeing distance of the horizon. You may now see around yourself but it is always the body that must communicate the change. (It is wise, in teaching, for the group to work simultaneously.)

6 - <u>Combining Areas</u>

It is interesting to combine all the areas by changing the area every two bars. This results in ten bars to the R and ten bars to the L. I usually divide the group into two and have one group work to the R while the second group observes, then the second group moves to the L while the first group observes the changes. This provides the opportunity to really see and feel the changes. Combining all the areas is very difficult and takes several attempts, but when finally conquered it is fascinating.

<u>Comment</u>:

1 - The difference between directional focus and area focus is in the use of the eyes. In directional, the eyes are on a fixed point and the space varies. In area, the eye-level varies but the space is specific.

2 - In the changing aspects of area focus we must not forget that the <u>quality</u> of the face changes along with the body. The face is part of the body. The increased breathing changes the entire body. If you really believe, what you are doing, it comes from deep within. The muscles of the face must change just as the eyes must change. You are living the moment. When you are sad, unconsciously the muscles of your face droop; if you are happy, they tend to turn up. Do not confuse <u>quality</u> with <u>making faces</u>. If the face remains a mask it means what is happening is external, mechanical.

3 - In the studio always hold the end of a phrase until all vibration of sound and self fade. Take a breath and hold that last moment. When on stage never let the audience see a

release of the intensity; hold that intensity until the curtain falls or the lights dim out.

4 - With the conscious use of area focus, you become aware of the tremendous importance space plays for you the performer. It is up to you to make the decision of the amount and kind of space you want.

5 - Never feel you are doing, even if it is a simple exercise; always feel you are being. With all senses alert, seek out your deepest feelings - make the immediacy of each moment come alive.

INNER FOCUS

Inner focus is a primary force. It is the element that transforms the performer into an artist. What is it? It is total concentration from the core of being.

This concentration demands an awareness - a need to dig deep and deeper in an endless search for your center. It is a form of self hypnosis. It entails a journey from outer self to inner self, a search, a discovery of the very kernel of being - an amalgam of all our life forces: senses, emotions, thinking, and experiences - filtered to become the essence of that center. All externals are peeled away; only the core remains. That core of being.

Inner focus lends an electric intensity to the performer. We call it presence. It is part of us, the part that binds all the elements of focus into one, that illumines - that reveals. It takes us to a higher level of consciousness - a sense of the immediate shadowed by a sense of timelessness. You must be so concentrated, so involved with the life on stage, that nothing else exists. Belief in what you are doing must be absolute. This belief concerns your emotions; nothing happens in life without some emotional involvement. It is your inner focus that makes you aware of all the nuances of emotional color. Coming from your center, it seeps through the pores of your body without trying. It is the feeling of emotion rather than emoting.

I do not like to use the word project, which involves an awareness of externals. The word I prefer is magnetize. The audience should come to you, the performer, and participate in that life on the stage. The only time I use the word "project" is in comedy, where addressing the audience is needed and you expect a response. However, if the comedy is based on satire you do not project, you magnetize.

It is the inner focus that binds the threads of a performance into a unified whole. In a dramatic work, when at times the action is taken by others, it is vital to maintain a sense of continuity. The concentration must never be lost: I call it the inner song. Even when you are not moving in space, time exists, and during that time you still move internally until the moment to move in space again arrives. In José Limón's "The Moor's

Pavane" the four characters are always on stage. It is a work based on <u>Othello</u> and consists of a series of court dances interspersed by dramatic episodes which develop the plot. During these episodes, there were moments when José Limón (Othello) and Lucas Hoving (Iago) were involved, while Betty Jones (Desdemona) and I (Emilia) were static, in some corner of the stage. For us it was not a matter of waiting until we resumed action. For inner continuity, we had to feel that we were not in the room but having a private conversation elsewhere, after which we re-entered to join our consorts. The same happened during all the various duets in the work. This kept us involved throughout the entire piece. Keeping all four characters on stage somehow gave the work an added dimension.

Sometimes there may be a distraction that causes you to lose the inner focus. Then, it is necessary to redirect your inner concentration and again find the center. Concentration is not a quality to turn on and off at will. It is the essence of true artistry; once it is lost and not regained the audience ceases to care. Inner focus gives credence to the <u>how</u> and not the <u>what</u> one does. With it, it is possible to stand perfectly still or move a little finger and hold the attention of the viewer; without it you may just as well be performing technical gymnastics.

Method

Rhythm: very slow 1 2 3 4 5 6 7 8 / 1 2 3 4 5 6 7 8

1 - <u>Improvs on Emotional Qualities</u>

<u>Frustration or anxiety</u>

Build from a mild state to the point of a shriek. The body must convey this in movement. This can be done more or less in one spot whether alone, or in a class, with the entire group working simultaneously. At first try, the results are usually fairly mild, partly because the inner focus is not strong enough and partly because of unconscious cliches. (Sometimes it is helpful to divide the group into two sections so that they may observe each other.)

Using the voice

Repeat the same problem with an actual vocal shriek, using your own timing for the shriek. It may sound like an insane asylum, but do not worry. The difference is startling. The voice creates an actuality that gives the movement an entirely different texture. The voice and movement are directly related to the self, indigenous to the body. There are no intermediary instruments needed to express that self. It is important to remember the feel of the body during the vocal shriek and reproduce that feel silently. (Again, by dividing the groups the performers see for themselves the enormous difference.)

Isolating limbs

Imagine lying in the sun absorbing the warmth. Feel alive, feel the sensuous heat of the sun, feel it on the skin. Try isolating a limb - a leg, an arm - while the rest of the body is always alive. The particular area plays a major role; the remainder is minor.

Sensing physically

Imagine water, being in it, splashing, touching it with a toe, being caressed by it. Is it cold? - shiver. Is it pleasant? - delight.

Sensing emotionally

Wait for someone to arrive with a sense of anticipation - fear. This is performed singly, each of you resolving the arrival in a personal way. It might turn out pleasantly or it might be terrifying. Live the experience!

Adding laughter

Almost any part of the body as well as the whole body is involved in laughter. Pick a specific kind of laughter from a giggle to a guffaw to a belly laugh. Travel across singly. Then, try it vocally with the movement. Again there is a great difference. The voice creates a reality of laughter that must be transferred to the body with the same sense of reality. Although the movement may seem stylized, the emotional quality will remain true.

Comment:

1 - Making the sound vitalizes the movement. Sound and movement are primary forms of expression. They are indigenous to the body. The body is our instrument.

2 - In working on inner focus it is necessary to go to the real life experience and then distill its emotion, its quality, until it is absorbed by total concentration, by utter belief, to become the center - the core of being.

MAGNETIC FOCUS

It is possible to convey a strong sense - of being drawn against your will, impelled, or repelled by a certain point, area, or person - by the use of the body, without necessarily the use of the eyes. This creates an awareness of a focal point on the floor or in space for the viewer as well as the performer.

The use of the body makes it obvious that the point, area, or person is of tremendous importance for the performer. That point, area, or person should be just as important for the viewer. You must capture the attention of that viewer. The performer is controlled by an external force, which I call magnetic. This is communicated by a particular quality of movement: drawn to it against the will - repelled by it pulling away - or propelled to it with a strong thrust. Until now the use of the eyes has been of great importance, but with magnetic focus it is the vital use of the body rather than the eyes that is absolutely essential. It is necessary to explore the full potential of that body movement in terms of resisting the force, of rebounding from it, or of needing to reach it. It can exist anywhere in space, at any height or depth; the motivation of the particular moment helps establish where the magnetic focus will be.

With these motivations, the inner focus allows you to discover movement never consciously used before. A new vocabulary is explored for each new problem. The technical exercises of the classroom (meant to train the muscles and align the body) are forgotten and totally unexpected body shapes and movement are the result. Since most of the exercises are based on improvisation, I find that no two people move alike, although they may have taken the same technique classes. The real person is revealed with a true sense of individuality. I am always fascinated by the wealth of creativity lying dormant in people. What they discover is as much a surprise to them as it is to me. Once discovered, the creative power becomes a challenge, an adventure, and a constant search for the self.

Counterbalance

In order to understand what body pull really entails (not just mechanical movement) it is necessary to convey a quality of great resistance. To achieve this counterbalance, pair off, hold both hands, and facing each other pull away by using the upper back with equal weight, counterbalancing each other. This allows you to feel what happens to your body, and feel the muscle intensity while pulling away very slowly as far as humanly possible without falling. It is vital to capture this feeling, which is needed for an imaginary pull. If you are working alone it is possible to hold on to any fixed object: a barre, the doorknob of a closed door, a post, or a washstand. All of the following exercises can be done singly, in pairs, or in groups, in the form of improvs.

1 - Drawn Against Will

Method

Establish a line from center - front of the room to center - back. This is the magnetic force. One part of the body will play a major role, the remainder will participate in a minor role. Each part of the body has a different feel and helps to investigate movement with different emphasis.

The arms

Resist the pull as you are drawn to the line; having passed it, pull away from the force with the sense of being held back by it. The body will telegraph the power of the magnetic center.

Make certain that you establish the power of that central area particularly when you reach the center and fight to pull away.

The head

We do not use the head enough, yet it can be a very vital source of movement and expression. The slightest tilt of the head can say many things emotionally as well as establish a character. The use of the head in magnetic focus helps us to discover a vast potential of head movement. With the sense of the head drawn against your will (the head being major, the remainder of the body minor) repeat the above. The entire body is always involved.

The hips

Hips can move sideways, backward, forward of the body, as well as rotate, as they are being drawn by the magnetic force. When pulling away from the center, you must be sure that the hips are held by the magnetic force. The power of pulling away must be as strong as that of being drawn against your will.

The legs

Now, use the legs as the dominant. When I ask what is felt the answer is usually <u>tension</u>. Tension is the wrong word; what is meant is muscle intensity (which will be discussed in detail when we get to dynamics). Tension locks the muscles and freezes the movement. Intensity is the energy we use in varying degrees to make the body feel vital, vibrant, alive. My favorite saying is, "Don't tense the muscle, sense the muscle."

Back, shoulders, feet

Repeating the original exercise formula, try using all the other parts of the body. They can contribute to the discovery of new and unusual movement. It is most important to remember that, although one part of the body is dominant the entire body is involved. It should not look like a study in isolated movement; which is a subject I will discuss when we get to movement texture.

2 - Repelled

Method

Try to reach a certain point or person but be repelled. There is attraction but a force flings you back so that a rebound of the movement occurs. It is interesting to do this in a circle with a group, spaced so that you will not collide. The magnetic point is the center of the circle. Using personal timing, work toward that point only to be forced back time and again.

3 - <u>Pulled Up</u>

Method

The body is pulled up against the will and you pull down, by resisting the force with any part of the body. It does not have to be distorted. It can be lyrical, slow, or fast depending on the motivation. At first, one tends to work with great intensity and that is good, but be aware of other possibilities and degrees of intensity.

4 - <u>Gravity: Resistance</u>

Resisting the pull of gravity involves falling in slow motion. You must resist the pull of gravity as long as possible until it is impossible to resist. Since you are struggling against the pull, the recovery will be fast. The result is quite fascinating. Most falls are done rapidly, with fast recoveries. The fall done very slowly introduces a strong emotional quality. It requires body control - not easy to achieve - and is rarely seen.

5 - <u>Gravity: Attraction</u>

You are attracted by gravity, - the fall will be fast and the recovery slow, which again introduces a new texture to the fall. Finally, you can establish two opposing points, which result in a fast fall and a rebound in recovery. When done with a group and ad lib timing, the result can be amazing.

BODY FOCUS

Body focus creates a heightened awareness of a particular part of the body, both for the performer and the viewer. This does not mean that only an isolated part is involved. Within a large movement, a small part of the body may be most important. A conscious awareness of that part becomes the focal point of that movement. However, the focal point can also be simply an isolated movement, for example, the rolling of the head or the rib cage movement in African dance, the hip movement in Hawaiian dance, or the hand movement of East Indian dance. All are examples of body focus. But these are part of an ethnic style in which the dancer has an inbred instinctive awareness of the focus.

No matter how small the movement may be it is vital to remember that the entire body is always involved. You are always the total performer. Every moment you are on stage you are performing, whether in stillness or in action.

Even in a technique class an awareness of body focus can reap great benefits. For instance a simple battement tendu forward will look quite different if there is a sense that the foot is pushing through sand - the wonder of the leg stretching from the thigh through the calf and the instep to the pointed toe; then the feel of pulling it back and placing the heel back to its fifth position. Rather than appearing mechanically exact it becomes vital, more vivid, alive. A port de bras should not be just an exact placement of arm positions, but should have the feel of using the air, shaping the space as well as the body. Almost every movement we make involves to a greater or lesser degree body focus. If you are aware of body focus in a technique class you learn more easily. The technique takes on an added dimension. To be aware is not enough. It should become a total body reflex.

Creatively, this area from the largest to the smallest allows you to dare new ways of moving. It broadens the potential possibilities of the body and releases you from depending on codified movement techniques. It allows you to stimulate the imagination and find your own identity.

Method

1 - <u>Improvs with Body Parts</u>

It is best to start with the larger limbs and diminish to the smallest possibilities such as eyebrows and mouth. (Improvs should be done solo, allowing each performer to move across the entire studio.) Free improv with the entire body involved.

Focus on the arms.

Elbows, then shoulders.

Legs, then knees.

Rib cage, then the back.

Head, wrists, fingers.

Ankles, toes, soles of the feet.

Ears, eyebrows, mouth.

<u>Comment</u>:

1 - In working on body focus I have discovered that we sometimes neglect certain areas of the body and often these are difficult to isolate. It is important to stress the upper torso (rib-cage and upper back). The ribs can be articulated sideways or rotated; the spine can curve, bend, or move successionally.

2 - Eyebrows present problems because most often the muscles controlling them are rarely used.

3 - Body focus and magnetic focus sometimes overlap, but one is usually dominant.

DRAMATIC FOCUS

I think that some performers do not realize how important it is to be aware of the dramatic potential in movement. Every dancer should be a good actor, just as every actor should know how to move well. I have found many important clues from <u>An Actor Prepares</u> by Constantin Stanislavski. It is possible to extract from this book what is important for the dancer-actor without getting too involved with the whole of his method.

The vital thing in performing a narrative ballet or a dramatic work, such as José Limón's "The Moor's Pavane", is to forget oneself. We must live the life of the character in the piece. We have to become that character and believe in that life on the stage. In the "Pavane" with all four characters always on stage two may be dominant while two may be tacit. At such tacit moments we created situations that would keep the characters alive. Not believing becomes playacting and is transparent. If we make the character real for ourselves, it will be real to others. We must believe - believe what we are doing. It takes exploring, digging into our innermost feelings, and into history whenever necessary.

If you are dancing a fictional character, it is up to you to create background for that character. Who was he or she before? Where did that person come from? What is happening to that person's life today and where will it go tomorrow? In this way you build a three-dimensional character. Now you know the reality of every moment you are on stage.

On the other hand, if you are to play a historic character it is most important to research the background of the character: the period, the style, the personal characteristics. You cannot just put on a costume and say, "I am that character." There will be no belief. All of this takes time, study, and hard work. But being an artist needs time, takes time, and throughout life will take more time. As you mature you discover greater nuance and depth in all that you do. To stop growing is to die as an artist.

Dramatic focus has several aspects, one of which is <u>relating to people</u>. It is most important to be aware on stage of people as people and not as things. Yet how many times have we seen a pas de deux where the woman has all the beautiful movement and the man is regarded simply as a support to show her off. He might as well be a broomstick. He does not relate to her as a woman. She does not relate to him as a man. She is busy looking at the audience with a broad smile. What is their relationship? Do they love each other or do they hate each other? Are they even aware of each other as people? It seems to me that a duet should have some emotional awareness, subtlety, color. When this happens I am thrilled emotionally, for they care about each other. I see a dance instead of a showpiece.

Another aspect is <u>relating to objects</u>, whether - real, symbolic, or imaginary. In dramatic focus you will explore all these kinds of relationships. You will be transformed from just a technical dancer to a dancer-actor, using your body with movement as your language.

Method

1 - People to People

Start with improvs involving two people. Decide who you are, what is your relationship, and how you feel about it. Make it come alive for yourselves and for the viewer. I call it playing to each other. How you relate to the other demands a certain response. The reaction cannot be decided in advance since it depends on the initial action. It is wise to designate who will initiate the action. The response can be quite surprising since it depends solely on inner feelings. It may be serious, tragic, or humorous. Very often a study that starts seriously may become humorous, and vice versa, by the way it is played back and forth. It is easier at first not to get too elaborate, but rather to concentrate on the problem.

Now, add one or two more people. Start with two, the others making separate entrances. This introduces a completely new element that changes the original dramatic idea by forcing the participants to respond. The idea can change from tragic to comic, from lyric to forceful, from joyful to rejection.

2 - <u>Timing</u>

Timing is one of the most important factors of dramatic focus. In the course of the people to people improvisations you will have discovered that some are believable while others are not. A shift from one emotion to another must not be arbitrary. You must give an emotion the time it takes to really feel it. The change must take place mentally and emotionally. It must be true. If you rush the time it takes to feel it within, it will be artificial. You will not be believed. Though nonverbal, there is a constant sense of almost verbal continuity within ("Oh how I love you," or "oh how I hate you"). You are living the life of that character. However, arbitrary change is good for comedy, since it is unexpected and consciously ridiculous, the sudden change becomes laughable.

Method

Hold a piece of cloth - a handkerchief, a towel, a scarf, or something similar. Stand in one place and look at it; turn slowly by crossing L foot over R and pivoting to the R. On completing the turn, allow the cloth to <u>drop</u> from the hands. It may be a memory or an association that is experienced that causes the cloth to drop. What is essential is that you take the time to relive the moment so that the dropping of the cloth conveys a strong emotional response.

Repeat the same movement, but this time the memory or association is one of anger or frustration and the cloth is <u>thrown</u> to the ground.

Repeat the movement, but this time the memory might be a tragic incident and results in <u>burying the face</u> in the cloth.

<u>Comment</u>:

Though this seems like a simple exercise the timing is crucial. Since the movement is minimal, you usually tend to rush it rather than giving the emotion the full time it takes to experience it. The true feeling must be the reason for the action. What you are doing is really happening to you. This simple problem with very little movement can have a powerful effect because the viewer becomes involved.

It will take time to find your self. The inner focus is essential for feeling the truth of an emotion; it cannot be faked. By constantly experimenting you become less self-conscious. The more you are involved with what is happening at your center the more you become the artist.

3 - Characterization

It is vital that you observe people in life, learn their movements and their idiosyncrasies and then stylize them: a mother, a father, a child, an old person, a haughty person, lovers, an evil person, an obsequious person, and so forth. If you have to play a character you must be believable in all the details. It is often helpful first to act out the character realistically. This makes the character come alive. Then having caught the very kernel of the character, convert it to dance movement.

Method

Choose a character and do a short improv in terms of that character.
Try improvs choosing characters of various kinds. Contrast the characters (if an old woman/man try a child).

Improv with more than one person, all playing specific characters,
to create a dramatic situation.

4 - Imaginary People

It is possible to perform a solo work and convey the impression that others are on stage. By using directional focus you can people the stage with as many or as few as the situation demands. Your dramatic relationship reveals to the viewer who the person or persons are in your imagination. Thus you can create a duet, a trio, or a room full of people. The eye level of the directional focus creates the size of these figures: tall or short or a child. The motivation helps to decide who the imaginary people are.

1 - Real Objects

Method

Improvise a short study, using as a reality whatever objects are available.

A chair is simply a chair.

A handkerchief is a handkerchief.

A box is a box.

A stepladder is a stepladder

2 - Symbolic or Association

In Anna Sokolow's "Rooms" each chair becomes a room where a particular life is lived. In an early solo, "Angelica," I used a ladder. The top was heaven where a dissatisfied angel flew. A decision was made to complete some unfinished business so I descended to earth by stepping down the ladder, completed my mission, and then up I went, to fly again, a very satisfied angel. In the use of objects symbolically the only limitation is your imagination.

3 - Imaginary objects

Method

Improv with an imaginary mirror.

Improv with an imaginary chair.

Improv handling an imaginary toreador's cape.

Improvs inventing any imaginary object you wish.

Comment:

An object need not be a factual presence but an imaginary object definable by movement. An imaginary crown can be placed on the head with the hands simulating holding it. A game of cards can be played by facing the palm of one hand toward the body while the other hand simulates in stylized movement card playing gestures.

Mimes employ imaginary objects constantly. Marcel Marceau's butterfly episode comes to mind. But let me remind you not to resort to mime. You must be constantly aware of the need to search for unexplored movement for your ideas. Improvisations using imaginary objects can be very rewarding.

The important element is to <u>believe</u> the object <u>exists</u> and make the viewer believe it as well.

PART 2 - DYNAMICS

Imagine being in a world where all the buildings were exactly alike, where there was only one color, where everyone spoke in the same tone, where everyone moved with the same rhythm, where there is no change. We would all be identical. Dynamics keeps interest alive. Without dynamics life would be unbearable. Yet we fail to see the absence of this vital quality in some of the arts. In recent years I have found the lack of dynamics in dance more and more prevalent. Dance has become a monotone of technical brilliance, an acrobatic tour de force rather than a work of art.

Dynamics Consists of Nuance, Color, Contrast

It is the bonemarrow of a performing artist, the very heartbeat of performance that makes it come alive, pulsating, spirit-stirring. Yet it is sadly neglected. Very often the choreographer who is pressed for time bypasses the dynamic potential.

It is often the performers' task to search and experiment and find the full dynamic possibility of the choreography. They become the interpreters who enrich the material with knowledge and imagination. This is why the same role done by various performers constantly changes in color and texture. What may seem dull at one viewing of a particular role may be a revelation at another. To learn the tremendous potential of dynamics with all of its subtlety is never-ending for it is ever-changing. After many years of performing the same role, one cannot be bored, for with maturity the concept grows in understanding and nuance.

Dynamics is controlled by energy.

Energy is controlled by breath.

Breath is the life-giving force.

My personal definition of dynamics has developed from constant experimentation to find what I feel are the basic essentials.

Dynamics in movement consist of the many varying gradations and relationships of three elements - time, intensity, and space range. These gradations contain all the possibilities from the smallest to the greatest.

Time may be slow to fast.

Muscular intensity may be weak to strong.

Emotional intensity may be gentle to powerful.

Space range may be small to great. Each part of the body has its own potential in space, just as the whole body has to entire space. What may be the very greatest space range for the head can be the smallest for the arm and even smaller for the leg. Space Range gradations are relative to different parts of the body.

Transition may be a gradual increase or decrease of any one or all the elements, or it may be a sudden change, such as an unexpected shift from one gradation to another of any one or all the elements.

The equivalent terms in music are accelerando and ritardando for time; crescendo and decrescendo for intensity; and subito for a sudden change, which includes immediate change from pianissimo to fortissimo as well as lento to allegro and vice versa.

Comment:

It is vitally important to understand that in using these various qualities each one is independent and does not automatically condition another. For instance, a small or great space range of the arm may use any gradation of muscular intensity: a small circle of the arm can have a great muscular intensity while a large circle might employ a small muscular intensity. They do not need to be parallel. It is the motivation that dictates the dynamic use, just as it does in focus.

Before starting it is essential to establish the proper body placement: the image to use is spread not lift. This spreading takes place in the rib cage. To test this, bend the palms back and place them on both sides of the ribs with the thumbs touching the ribs in back and the remaining fingers touching the ribs in front. Take a deep breath so the palms spread apart evenly front and back. Now release the breath and hold the ribs by use of the muscles. This may be difficult at first since the muscles may not have been trained for expansion in this area, but by repeating the breathing-and-holding it will be possible to expand and hold the ribs with no effort.

I also give the image of the chest being a shelf. The neck and head rest on this shelf. On the underside of the shelf are two hooks from which the legs hang. A third image is that of a "T": the crossbar is the shoulders, which press down toward the chest; the vertical stem starts at the center of the head and travels through the spine. When this placement becomes the norm, you find buoyancy, better elevation, more lung space for breathing, and better balance. It should be the dancer's permanent stance. In <u>lifting</u>, the ribs are usually tilted, which creates lordosis in the arch of the lower back. <u>Spreading</u> the rib cage pulls the stomach muscles in and keeps the spine in alignment. Furthermore broadening the chest cavity diminishes the appearance of width in the hips.

Method

For the sake of experimentation I have tried to create a very dull phrase to see what happens when the various principles of dynamics are applied. My motivation is simply to touch, to feel space in various directions.

The phrase consists of four bars with a count of 6 for each bar. From the starting position each bar uses 3 counts for the initial movement and 3 to return to the starting position. What I call the starting position is the body poised, ready to move.

1   STARTING POSITION

All movement must give the sense of feeling air, exploring planes

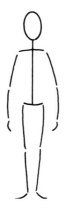

2 - Extend right foot to right; extend right arm to right, palm facing front, left arm bent at elbow across chest palm facing body; slight plié left leg 1 2 3. Back to starting position 4 5 6

3 - Raise right knee bent forward - left arm reaches up through bent elbow, palm facing front - head slightly tilted up 1 2 3. Back to starting position 4 5 6.

4 - Shift balance to right leg demi-plié, left leg croise back low attitude, both arms open side slight down diagonal, palms front, head turned to left 1 2 3. Back to starting position 4 5 6.

5 - Step forward on left leg to fourth position left knee bent, weight forward, right leg straight - both arms bent, elbows close together; on forward move, circle hands forward as if touching the rim of a bowl 1 2 3. Back, circling hands toward body as touching the rim of a bowl 4 5 6.

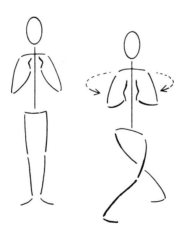

This is the basic phrase with which you will experiment. A very dull movement becomes more and more interesting as the different aspects of dynamics are layered upon it.

It will take a great deal of concentration and exploration until you will feel at ease. The variations used can be applied to any phrase and you should feel free to create your own phrase if you so please. I present this as an example of how to go about discovering the infinite possibilities that dynamics offers and suggest that after becoming familiar with the material, an actual phrase or phrases from existing repertoire be used. Look for all the many ways of enhancing the material by introducing the various gradations of all three areas of dynamics. It is of great value to see how different dancers interpret the same phrase and how that phrase differs in impact on the viewer.

TIME

Method

1 - Time Change

(Always repeat on opposite side)

Do all phrases in two counts, holding 3 and 6.

Do all phrases in one count, holding 2 3 and 5 6

Syncopate move on "&" of 1&, hold 2 3 and 4&, hold 5 6.

By shortening the time in which the movement is performed it becomes sharper. The overall phrase length remains the same.

Time change each bar

First bar: open out 1 2, hold 3 close 4, hold 5 6

Second bar: raise arm and leg 1, lower 2 3 4 5 6

Third bar: open arms, leg to attitude 1 2 3, hold 4, down 5, hold 6

Fourth bar: hold 1, move leg to fourth circling hands, forward &2 3, return hold 4, moving leg back, hands circling back, & 5 6

SPACE RANGE

1 - Space Change To begin, work in small, medium, and great range.

Do entire original phrase first in great range, second in medium range, third in small range.

Combine first bar, great + second bar, medium + third bar, small and fourth bar, great.

2 - <u>Combining Time and Space Range</u>

To the time change pattern add the changing space range pattern.

To same time change pattern, reverse space range pattern to small, medium, great, small. As these changes are made you can see how the quality of the phrase changes by changing the space range. The movement is becoming visually more and more interesting. It is possible to invent as many variations as one pleases.

INTENSITY

1 - <u>Muscular</u>

An important thing to remember is not to confuse the word tension with intensity. Tension locks the muscles, freezing them. This kills the movement unless this is demanded by the motivation. Tension is the opposite of intensity. Intensity vitalizes, depending on the amount of energy you use.

<u>Do not tense the muscle, sense the muscle.</u>

Method

Rhythm: slow 1 2 3 4 5 6 7 8

that is the fuel that feeds energy? It is <u>breath</u>. More breath, more energy; less breath less energy. Let us experiment with breath.

Raise both arms to the side while breathing short breaths in out. Feel like you are pushing the air by trying to increase the muscle intensity. It seems impossible since each time you breathed out you lost energy.

Repeat the exercise, but this time take one long breath for the duration of the eight counts. The constant breath feeds the energy, allowing for an increase in the muscle intensity. As you lower the arms and breathe <u>out</u> slowly, you find the intensity diminishes. However, if you start with the arms up and breathe <u>in</u> as you lower them, the intensity increases.

The size of the movement does not influence the power, a very small movement may have a strong muscle intensity and vice versa. The energy used is the deciding factor. Using the basic phrase with the time change and initial space range change, add the muscle intensity - strong, medium, weak, strong. Experiment with variations of muscle intensity, such as weak, medium, strong, weak. (When working with a group it is interesting to divide the group into two units, so that one group observes while the other moves.)

2 - Emotional

This is a vast field not only because of the infinite variety of emotions, but also because each emotion has its own gradations depending on the motivation. We can be happy that we have achieved an important goal in life (powerful gradation) or we can be happy because we have just received a compliment (gentle gradation). The degree of emotional intensity in anger will vary from a slight insult to a violent confrontation. I suggest making a list of the major emotions and under each category list all the minor ones relating to that category. This can reveal the many possibilities of dynamic nuance within a single emotion.

Method

With the time and space range phrase set up four gradations of a single emotion: powerful, medium, gentle, powerful.

With the time and space range phrase take the emotional gradations in reverse order: gentle, medium, powerful, gentle. This phrase will have an entirely different impact from the first.

With the time and space range phrase try various emotions and suggest the motivations for the change. Sinister, joyous, shy, loving. Although it is rather arbitrary to change emotions within a four bar phrase, you can make it possible by creating a small scenario: You expect someone to arrive whom you hate. Instead a good friend enters. At first you feel sinister; now with the appearance of a friend you are joyous, shy, loving.

Comment:

At first you may feel slightly self-conscious. However it soon becomes very satisfying to be involved with emotional color. It will be evident in the entire body, even the face (I do not mean emoting). When joyous, the face takes on a glow; when shy it is more contained; when angry, the facial muscles always react, they tighten; when sad, they unconsciously droop. The change comes from the inner experience, the inner focus. The feelings must always come from the deepest center so that the entire body, not just the face reflects these feelings. Dynamics has made the original dull phrase interesting, more provocative; the phrase, which began with simply feeling space, takes on dramatic overtones because of the emotional color.

COMBINING DYNAMIC ELEMENTS

It may take some time to absorb all the fascinating possibilities of dynamics. Like focus it must become so ingrained in the performer's consciousness that it is there as reflex action, not as a mechanical analysis. It must become an integral part of the performer, so that the technique will not dominate. Then there will be a blend of all the factors resulting in a unified whole. When I listen to Arthur Rubinstein play Chopin with infinite emotional sensitivity and color I am moved. It is difficult to understand why so many performers neglect giving emotional color enough attention. Those who do are easily singled out as very special. This is something you must find for yourself.

Method

1 - Improvs

Create a short phrase of about four bars.

First do it simply with no dynamic color.

Repeat the same phrase with a time change.

With time change add a space range change.

Add a muscular intensity change.

Finally add an emotional intensity change.

Comment:

Usually, the muscular intensity parallels the emotional intensity but there are exceptions. For instance, we may be so shocked that we faint. This demands very powerful emotional intensity coupled with the weakest muscle intensity. Or if one is slightly drunk and feeling great, the muscular intensity is weak with a loss of muscular control. All human beings feel emotion of some kind and it constantly varies. Without emotion we would simply be puppets. As an artist it is important to reveal all the possible nuances and subtleties of emotion without exaggeration. Exaggeration is actually a non-emotion, since it is put on like a cloak to mask the lack of the true inner quality.

Experiment with the various colors. Try every possibility. Include any combination of the above and repeat improvs, varying all possible aspects of dynamics. Think of what happens in life, what happens to others, as well as yourself, and stylize it in movement. Try paralleling muscular and emotional intensity. Try them in opposition, which very often can be used for humor or satire.

TRANSITIONS

Method

Any one or all the elements of dynamics involve transitions that are either gradual or sudden.

1 - Time: Gradual Increase

Alternate a full circle of the arms front of body: 1 2 3 4, then on 1 2 3, then on 1 2 , then on 1, and finally double-time (1&). This can be done with any part of the body.

2 - Time: Gradual Decrease

Reverse by starting with double-time, ending with 1 2 3 4 .

3 - Time: Sudden Change

Switch from 1 2 3 4 to 1. Though the movement is basically in the arms, the entire body must be involved.

4 - Space Range: Gradual Increase

Rhythm: slow 1 2 3

Without changing time value circle R leg and arm in front of body L to R: small, then medium, then great.

Repeat opposite side.

5 - Space Range: Gradual Decrease

Reverse the range great, medium, small. Both sides.

6 - Space Range - Sudden Change

Circle from greatest to smallest, smallest to greatest, omitting medium.

Comment:

You will find that by varying the space range of the same movement you retain interest. Never forget the words nuance and contrast. The immense difference between area focus and space range is that area focus deals with the inner concept of where we are in space, no matter what the movement may be, while space range deals with the external shape of a phrase which changes the appearance of the movement.

7 - Intensity (muscular): Gradual Increase

Raise the right knee and gently tap the sole of the foot on the floor. Increase the muscle intensity as the tap continues. The contact with the floor will increase in sound. But it is also possible to increase muscle intensity without changing the sound. This often occurs with rebound, which will be discussed later.

8 - Intensity (muscular): Gradual Decrease

Repeat above, starting with maximum intensity; decrease as tapping continues to minimum intensity.

9 - Intensity (muscular): Sudden Change

Shift foot tap from maximum to minimum intensity without any transition. Repeat in reverse. The muscular intensities should be tried with various parts of the body as well as with the entire body. Experiment with sudden shifts in gradation. Many unusual effects will result.

10 - Intensity (emotional): Gradual Increase of a Single Emotion

This is more difficult, because the change must be gradual, subtle, and convincing; too much change can lead to emoting.

Pick a motivated emotion and improvise, based on the emotion and really believing in it. Take anger: someone has circulated a derogatory remark. Meet the imaginary person. An argument develops to the point of near violence. Feel the mounting anger and make the viewer recognize it.

11 - Intensity (emotional): Gradual Decrease of a Single Emotion

Pick any emotion. Start at the most powerful and create a reason for decreasing the emotion.

12 - Intensity (emotional): Sudden Change

Pick any emotion. Shift via the motivation from gentle to powerful or powerful to gentle, without any transition. Experiment with various emotions. The sudden change can reap comic results.

Learn to know yourself.

Pauline Koner, Improvization (Leningrad, 1936)

Pauline Koner
Photographer : Herbert Migdol

Area Focus : Solitude and Dynamics : Emotion (Powerful)
Pauline Koner in *The Farewell* (Part IV The Last Farewell)
Choreographer : Pauline Koner
Photographer : Peter Basch

Area Focus : Out of Doors
Pauline Koner, Improvisation

Area Focus : Horizon
Pauline Koner and Martha Curtis
Improvisation (1977)
Photographer : Jack Mitchell

Dramatic Focus
Pauline Koner and José Limón in *La Malinche* (1948)
Choreographer : José Limón
Photographer : Walter Strate

Dynamics and Focus : Various Emotional Gradations
Pauline Koner
Photographer : Gerda Peterich

Dramatic Focus : Characterization
(from left to right) Pauline Koner, Lucas Hoving, José Limón and Betty Jones
in José Limón's *The Moor's Pavane* (1949)
Photographer : Jorge Gutierrez

Dynamics : Various Gradations
Dramatic Focus : Characterization
The Pauline Koner Dance Consort in III Movement of Flight, *Flight of Fancy*
(from left to right) Patricia Casey, Keith Sabado, Martha Curtis and Paco Garcia
Choreographer : Pauline Koner
Photographer : David Groover

Dynamics : Muscular Intensity (Strong)
Pauline Koner Dance Consort in *Cantigas* (1978)
with Zane Rankin (kneeling), Paco Garcia and Michael Freed
Choreographer : Pauline Koner
Photographer : David Groover

Dynamics : Emotional Intensity (Great)
Pauline Koner in *La Malinche* (1948)
Choreographer : José Limón
Photographer : Walter Strate

Movement : Texture
Pauline Koner in *The Solitary Song* (1962)
Choreographer : Pauline Koner
Photographer : Peter Basch

Movement Texture : Suspension
Pauline Koner in *Ravel Waltz* (1941)
Choreographer : Pauline Koner
Photographer : Gerda Peterich

Props : *Long Cloth*
Gina Vidal and Gyula Pandi in *Poéme* (1968)
Choreographer : Pauline Koner
Photographer : William Beck

Costume : Caftans, Snapped Up
The Pauline Koner Dance Consort in *Cantigas* (1978)
Choreographer : Pauline Koner
Dancers : Karen Shields, Valorie Farias, Paco Garcia and Zane Rankin
Photographer : David Groover

Costume : Skirts
Pauline Koner in *In Memoriam* (1944)
Choreographer : Pauline Koner
Photographer : Gerda Peterich

PART 3 - MOVEMENT TEXTURE

Until now we have been discussing dynamics in terms of gradations which are essential for color and contrast. But above and beyond that there is the question of <u>how</u> we move. There are certain qualities that offer fascinating possibilities for infinite variety, interest, and nuance. To be an artist it is necessary to explore, to grow, to discover the full gamut of movement texture: I do not pretend that these qualities are the only ones. On the contrary, there are as many possibilities as there is imagination.

WEIGHT

One of the important qualities discovered during the beginnings of modern dance was weight. This quality lent each movement an importance that had not been evident in classical dance and that became a distinguishing factor of early modern dance. I don't think we were consciously aware of weight, it was simply a way of moving. Only now that it has almost disappeared do we recognize it as weight.

Today, when I see a revival of a modern dance work - a work that once made me tremble with excitement - I sometimes find it pallid, dull, boring. What is wrong? It is not that the work in itself is dull, but how it is performed. The technique of the dancers is brilliant, yet it is still boring. In trying to determine what is wrong I constantly come back to the realization that the missing quality is weight. There is much discussion about it by modern dancers who oddly enough are typed as the classic modern dance (the title seems rather ridiculous for how can one be classic and modern at the same time?).

What is weight?

It is an awareness of air as a form of density rather than a vacuum.

It is a use of muscle intensity with the variation of energy that controls the intensity.

It is the use of breath as an integral part of movement.

It is the involvement of the total body, although the movement may be an isolated part.

It is the synthesis of mind, body, and energy.

It is an inner conviction that each moment is important.

49

How was it lost?

As modern dance developed, it was recognized that more speed, elevation, and facile leg work was needed in the technique. After establishing its own identity apart from classical ballet, modern dance was able to incorporate the qualities inherent in ballet: lightness, buoyancy, a defiance of gravity - the realm of the air. Technical facility in modern dance has now reached a point beyond all expectation. Dancers have extensions that reach toward the sky - six o'clock arabesques - and they can fly across the stage with grands jetes. In their efforts to excel, one of the seeds of their origin, weight, has been forfeited. At the same time, classical ballet incorporated some qualities basic to modern dance: floor falls, and crawls of all description - the realm of the earth. But ballet, without having experienced weight, lost nothing in its use of earth qualities.

As a result what we see in modern dance is brilliant dancing that is movement making, rather than making movement. Strength is now the watchword. A sense of weight is rare. The beauty and power of simplicity, of organic movement involving the entire body from its deepest core, has given way to external slickness. But there is no reason why dancers today cannot broaden their horizons to include both the realm of the air and the realm of the earth.

The degree of muscle intensity needed for weight depends on resistance. We feel this when we swim. Water has density and we push or pull against it to travel forward, resisting its density. However, we sometimes forget that air also has density. We can rest on it, push, pierce, cut, grasp, embrace, and mold it. Each of these actions demands a different degree of muscle intensity created by our energy. For example, when our arms rest on the air very little energy is required, but if we press down on the air we should feel the resistance - greater energy is needed and the muscle intensity is increased. It is the sense of the resistance against our pressure that gives the movement weight. For this we depend upon energy fueled by breath. In The Language of Dance, Mary Wigman wrote, "Breath is the mysterious great master who reigns unknown and unnamed behind all and everything."

Method

1 - <u>Weight</u>

Raise arms sideways slowly in one breath, without feeling any resistance. You will find that very little breath is needed.

Now try the same movement, feeling a resistance to the air   (pushing the air), while taking short inhalations and exhalations. Try to increase the intensity. It seems impossible.

Repeat the same movement resisting the air as you take a deep breath. The muscle intensity grows. Lower the arms while breathing out. The intensity will diminish and vice versa.

<u>Comment</u>:

It is important to keep constantly in mind the sense of space as density, to which all movement must relate. Opening the arms is opening the space; closing the arms may be gathering the space or embracing the space; a slashing movement cuts the space. An awareness of space is essential and muscle intensity must be felt in every part of the body - the legs, the back, the head, even the fingers, every part that moves. Dance is movement that exists in space and time. Use that space consciously.

If we give in to gravity in a fall there is very little or no   resistance, so that the muscle intensity is weak. Resist gravity in the fall (the fall becomes slow motion} and the intensity of the muscle becomes strong.

However muscle intensity alone is not the answer. It is only   the means, part of the technique. What is most surprising in sensing weight is that it has nothing to do with a dancer's external appearance. One can be tall or short, heavy or fragile, and still convey a sense of weight. It comes from within and depends on the motivation that dictates the movement, from the lightness of a lyric moment to the power of a dramatic gesture. Motivation helps you to phrase, color, and contrast movements; qualities often lacking in our technique oriented dancers of today.

The inner awareness of the <u>what</u> and the <u>how</u> in making a movement meaningful is basic. The sense of weight is a matter of mind and body. Some dancers have an instinctive feeling of weight. When they move we recognize it immediately. But it is also possible to achieve it by using motivated muscle intensity in its infinite gradations. It takes practice and experimentation until it becomes an integral part of your concept. When that happens you have rediscovered this essential lost quality of weight.

POINT OF PULSE

An increase and decrease of energy, which may last longer than a single beat without changing the time duration of the movement, creates a pulse within the movement. I think of a point of pulse as a surge, an energy curve. It can occur in slow or medium-fast movement. The breath is in, sustained, and slowly released, depending on the pulse. Do not confuse point of pulse with accent which happens on the beat; pulse carries beyond the beat (1&).

Method

Rhythm: slow 1 2 3 4

Circle R arm forward from L to R with the pulse on the first beat 1 2 3 4

Repeat four times.

Repeat with the left arm.

Change pulse to the second beat 1 2 3 4 (R,L) four times.

Change pulse to the third beat 1 2 3 4 (R,L) four times.

Change pulse to the fourth beat 1 2 3 4 (R,L) four times.

Now with R arm do four circles 1 2 3 4 changing the pulse to the next beat on each circle.

Repeat with left arm.

If four people are available and each one takes a different count for the pulse, the result is amazing. The phrase becomes a fascinating canon. Keep in mind that point of pulse must be used with discretion. Any movement texture if overused can become a cliche.

Comment:

Depending on the initial speed point of pulse may last only one beat in a slow tempo or extend beyond the beat in a faster tempo.

It can be used only in slow to moderately fast tempo. At a presto tempo it loses the pulse and becomes an accent.

You will find that using point of pulse at different moments changes the texture of that movement as well as the emotional quality.

Using the above method, experiment with the legs, the head in a circular motion, and any part of the body that can adapt to pulse. Most Far Eastern dancers move with this quality. It is ingrained in their movement style. Whether I acquired it while working with the Japanese dancers Michio Ito and Yeichi Nimura or had it instinctively (some dancers do) I will never know. It is one of the qualities that can be introduced without changing the concept of the choreographer and that differentiated my movement from the style of the José Limón Company. It was the first time I became consciously aware of this difference and it took me a long time to analyze what I really did. Finally point of pulse seemed the best way to describe it.

It lends a special kind of color that etches the movement in space, and though it often may not be recognizable you feel the difference. The movement takes on a breathing vitality, a living entity. Try introducing it to a known phrase and see what happens. In experimenting add a vocal sound to the pulse, letting the sound come from within. The voice often helps tremendously in realizing the full potential of point of pulse.

ACCENT

An attack, a stress, or an emphasis at a particular point of movement. An accent that occurs on a single beat may happen at any speed. The breath is sharp and may be in or out.

SUSTAINED MOVEMENT

This is the continuous flow of movement without pulse or accent in a given time length with normal breathing (in and out). This can happen at any speed. However, sometimes very fast movement may become sharp, thus losing the quality of constant flow.

<h2 style="text-align:center">SUSPENSION</h2>

Movement that grows by the timing of breath. This creates the quality of being poised or hanging in midair. Suspension is controlled by breath timing and must be recreated with each new breath; the longer the breath the greater the suspension. It is essential that you work to devlop your breathing capacity in order to get the full benefit of suspension.

Method

Rhythm: 1 2& 3 4

In a zigzag pattern across the room. Start downstage left with

L foot 1 2-& 3 4 diagonal to upstage right.

Suspend, turning 1/4 turn left on L foot 4 raising R arm, head to right facing up toward arm, right leg barely touching the floor. Do not try to hold the turn in a balanced position. It must be total suspension, pulling up to half-toe in 1/4 turn left. Build a breath phrase on 4. On releasing breath fall forward on the R leg on 1 2-& 3 4. Travell downstage diagonal.

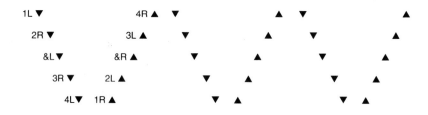

Keeping the second leg close to the floor avoids holding a balanced attitude. The goal is to take a longer breath on each count of 4. This develops the suspension and makes the rhythm uneven since the fourth beat is held, as a fermata is in music.

Suspension does not necessarily mean up. The body may be in any position as long as it depends on the breath for timing.

Rhythm; 1& 2 3 4

Run forward (R, L, R) 1& 2 swing L leg, both arms and body forward on 2.

Holding L leg in forward attitude, swing arms and body to a

semi-backbend suspension on R half-toe 3 hold 4. It is important that the back swing is counterbalanced by the standing leg pushing forward into the hip. The greater the counterbalance the more thrilling the suspension. Legs alternate.

Always be certain that the movement back does not become a static balance. In suspension the body is always in movement.

Suspension can also exist with the focus down; you can appear to be hanging in the upper back while the head and shoulders focus down. Experiment with various parts of the body adding turns as well. Suspension is one of the most exciting and beautiful textures for it stretches time as well as the body. It soars in constant movement. It never freezes.

REBOUND

A bouncing back from an initial movement. This reaction changes in proportion to the energy and muscular intensity of the initial movement. Rebound can occur in any direction and in any part of the body. A rebound cannot be an initial movement, it can be only a result. The use of rebound is refreshing in that the degree and variety achieved is never-ending.

Method

Try rebounds with arms, legs, head, torso, hips, feet, and hands. Use various directions: out, in, up, down.

Use great energy for initial movement. This will cause the rebound to be great

Use less energy for the initial movement. The rebound will be proportionately less.

The Doris Humphrey technique depends a great deal on suspension and rebound. Percussionists and conductors also rely on rebound.

MOVEMENT OVERTONES

Although a movement has stopped in space it should always convey a sense of vitality, of the air still vibrating. You may have stopped in <u>space</u>, but you must continue to move in <u>time</u>. When a tone in music is held, the vibrations continue to rise in a given formula inaudible to the normal ear. These are called overtones. In movement you must retain an energy flow and intensity even in stillness. You must think you are still moving. This prevents a frozen appearance - a living photograph.

Method

Raise one or both arms up, reaching into space, and on reaching the apex feel the movement still going onward.

Repeat, this time on reaching the apex, stop. Freeze the movement. By consciously stopping the sense of moving there is a difference in the' feel as well as a visible difference. It is the difference between the life and the death of a movement.

ISOLATIONS

We sometimes forget how many parts of the body we have and how mobile they can be. Isolating them can produce a variety of new and unusual effects. However, it is wise to remember motivation even as simple as "I want to create interest in that part." There is a wealth of movement to be discovered with one head, two arms, two legs, the torso, ribs, hips, buttocks, knees, ankles, wrists, fingers, eyebrows, and even the mouth - possibilities very often neglected. Simply turning the head at a particular moment can have tremendous significance, both emotionally and dramatically. It seems to me that the head is not used enough.

In José Limón's "La Malinche" I did nothing but a slow walk, holding high in my right hand a large yellow kerchief. All I did was tilt my head down to the right shoulder, then raise my left palm to my breast. The impact of inner anguish for this lament was intense. The isolation said everything. I have talked about body focus earlier and it is important to incorporate it in isolation when needed.

The hands are also very expressive and are often forgotten. However discretion is advisable. Too much isolation can fragment movement and make it look fidgety. The use of isolation is important for contrast rather than a style. Isolation is basically the realm of the choreographer but often the performer and the choreographer are one and the same.

Method

Improvise phrases moving in space and introduce two moments of isolated movement. These may be structured (i.e., a head and a knee). Choose your own.

Improvise a phrase using only isolations.

Improvise two phrases, the first using two isolations, the second continuous isolations. Compare the various effects, both good and bad.

FLUTTERS, TREMORS, SHIVERS

Flutters are achieved by rapid movement of the hands up and down or a rolling from the wrist. This requires a counterpoint of maximum energy and muscle intensity in a minimum space range. The vertical movement can also happen in the feet from the ankle. A flutter is larger and slower than a tremor.

Method

Rhythm: 1 2 3 4 5 6 7 8

Flutter R hand in a triplet to each beat.

Flutter L hand.

Flutter both hands.

A tremor is basically a flutter but the motion is faster, tighter, and done in a smaller space range.

R hand 4/16 to a beat.

L hand.

Both hands simultaneously.

Shivers: the entire body trembles.

Comment:

These textures are best used when motivated: flutter might be leaves falling or a heartbeat; tremor might be excitement or nervous agitation; a shiver could be fear, cold or ecstasy. Flutters, tremors, and shivers must be used with discretion. They sometimes may be used to good effect for humor.

STILLNESS

Dancers tend to move more in recent years. The present trend is to glorify technique. The criterion seems to be, "I must be brilliant, I must be strong." They seem to have forgotten the impact of stillness. There was a time when dancers were so busy being still they almost forgot to move. That too was wrong. Neither extreme is desirable.

Contrast is one of the most important elements for maintaining the interest of the viewer. As sharpness is to soft movement and strength to weak movement, stillness is the ultimate to any movement. No matter how brilliant you are without some contrast the viewer stops caring. It is taken for granted. Monotony is hypnotic - contrast is stimulating. The impact of stillness depends on the timing. There is no formula, for the stillness must relate in timing to what has preceded it. Only the inner focus and practice determine this timing.

Method

In groups of two or three, improvise movement without stopping.

Repeat improvisation and at any time hold, then continue.

Move fast, stop and hold; suddenly start again with fast tempo.

Start slowly and continue; stop and hold; start slowly. Repeat. Start slowly and increase tempo; stop and hold suddenly. Repeat.

Start quickly and decrease tempo to a stop and hold. Repeat.

Comment:

These exercises may be tried on a walking and running ground base or on improvised phrases. Each variation will demand a difference in the timing of the stillness. What is important to notice is that each of you will have a slightly varied sense of the timing for the held moment.

Summary:

Each of you must rely on the center of your being, that inner intensity that is the seed of the self. That is precious. It must be nourished and cherished. It allows the imagination to soar, to create new movement rather than to rely on a studied technique.

Allow yourselves the challenge of <u>risk</u> for without taking a risk you may never discover your full potential. Taking a risk means reaching as far as you can but with control; otherwise it might lead to serious accidents. But before taking that risk you must find your true center and know how far to depart from that center to take the risk. You may take a risk in balance, in the use of space, or in falls, but it is essential to be extremely conscious of each movement - each moment of risk.

Above all you should never be satisfied with what you have done. Constant growth, finer nuance, always the need to be better the next time is what creates the true artist.

II

SECONDARY ELEMENTS

THE CRAFT

PART 4 - PROPS, FABRIC, COSTUME

Although I call the craft the secondary elements, they are no less important for the performer as an artist. The primary elements deal with the inner person, the secondary with the outer person. This component examines the technique of manipulating various props with facility and assurance. It involves anything from stage levels; (ramps, steps, platforms) to smaller props (cubes, benches, chairs) to hand props (fans, hoops, Chinese ribbons, elastic, even umbrellas). It explores the use of cloth of various lengths and textures as well as costumes with long skirts or trains. There is also the area of bows, entrances and exits, and behind-the-scenes activity. With practice you can avoid the problem of spending time on these externals while learning a new work and can concentrate instead on the content of the work. What is important is not having to worry about mechanics, by being totally prepared.

One of the reasons Doris Humphrey, Martha Graham, and Charles Weidman often used props and handled them so magnificently is the in-depth experience they had during their years with the Denishawn company. Props were an essential in many of their works. To have seen Martha use a piece of fabric for whatever dramatic purpose she needed was to experience the truth and power of its use. Today technique classes are purely physical, there is very little chance for exploring the use of props. I regard it necessary to study the craft - vital to being a total artist.

All props may be approached in one of several ways, depending on the motivation. For example, as a reality a chair is a chair; as a symbol it may be a cage or a gateway or an obstruction. It may also be a memory. It can trigger an association of a past experience. Finally, it can be used for its design in space.

STAGE PROPS

1 - <u>Levels</u>

Working with levels requires certain body adjustments which, with practice, become reflex action. There must always be a sense of security and ease. If you reveal the mechanics or show effort the viewer begins to worry. To travel up a ramp you need to lean forward for impetus; travelling down you need to tilt slightly back. I found this to be true when I had to work on raked stages. Walking up steps or rising to a level of any height, the body must be buoyant: the body and full weight should be on the foot that leads, pushing down and using the energy in the thigh muscle to pull upward. On the other hand, in descent, the full weight is kept on the back leg, while the leading leg reaches down. It is vital to feel the lower level or step before shifting weight, which prevents falling off. All of us do this as a reflex every time we walk up and down steps. But many times stage designers, cramped for space, must change the proportions of steps.

<u>Comment</u>:

It is important to check at each performance to see that the props are in the correct spot and that they are secure, (rubber on the base gives them traction).

Never step up on a level too close to the edge. Stepping on the very edge of a bench may raise the opposite end, with dire results.

If a pattern travels on a bench do not travel so far that there is no space left to finish the phrase. Learn to space the movement by adjusting the size of your steps.

A bench offers all kinds of possibilities besides stepping up and down and moving across it. You can sit on it and bend back toward the audience, pivot on it, roll off it, use it any way you wish. You must learn how to handle these moves mechanically.

If you need a hand for support, then a way of concealing it is necessary. Usually use the upstage hand.

If the stage is slick and there is no traction on stepping up, be sure that your weight comes down vertically: otherwise there is the danger of pushing the level on stepping up.

The aim is always to protect your safety, yet never reveal the mechanics. These are the secrets of performing that are absorbed by experimenting. You must always be conscious of your body and of every move you make, but never lose inner focus. Never lose sight of the fact that the dance is more important than the prop.

Long bench, 6 to 8 feet minimum

Place bench in center of space. Since no two stages are the same, learn to pace a phrase in relation to that space: steps must be longer or shorter. Practice the pattern on the floor level before working on the bench.

Method

Rhythm: 1 2& 3 4 5 6 7 8 / 1 2 3 4

Starting with R foot, run toward bench 1 2& 3.

With R foot step up on bench 4

Travel to center of bench L 5 R 6

En balançoire L back 7 front 8

Continue on bench L 1 R 2

Step down on L 3, R 4.

Repeat on opposite side.

Note   * Be near enough to bench to step up on it.

       * Make sure the balançoire is done where enough space remains to finish phrase properly.

       * Overcome fear of height so that you do not lose balance on narrow bench.

       * On descending brush leg on edge of bench for security.

       * Never clump down: land on ball of foot into heel.

Repeat same phrase but replace en balançoire with half turn upstage on L foot 7 8

Step backward R 1 L 2

Descend backward on R 3

Turn half downstage 4.

Repeat on opposite side

Add full turn upstage L 7 R 8

Step L forward 1

Turn half downstage on R foot 2

Descend backward L 3 half turn downstage R 4

Repeat same phrase replace the en balançoire with any kind of suspension and descend in any manner.
Repeat opposite side.

Comment

Since bench is narrow you must be very secure in holding the suspension by remaining on two feet. Later, you can raise a leg and add arms so that the phrase becomes more and more a dance phrase.

Note   * Be sure the breath is used for suspension.

      * To fall out of the suspension more space must be allowed at the far end of the bench so that you do not fall off.

      * Take smaller steps before the suspension to compensate.

Improvs on bench, reverse turns for a twining look.

Add two other levels - cubes or boxes - in asymmetric spacing. Leap onto the level. Do a movement pattern and jump off.

Add motivation; perhaps it is a journey. Decide the emotional color. The improv may include two or three people spacing the time accordingly. The improv should be played from one to another, but always with awareness of the levels as an integral part of the action.

Comment:

It is useless to do movement on the floor behind a level: it will be lost.

2 - STEPS

With limited stage space, steps may not have normal depth. In that case you must place the foot diagonally on going up or down. This ensures safety for if you place the foot directly forward, the back half may be off the step. When steps are available, try various rhythms and speeds ascending and descending.

3 - LADDERS

Ladders are a fascinating prop to work on. They lend themselves particularly to symbolic use. The tentlike shape, the flat top, the steps, the openings between the steps, offer many interesting possibilities.

Ladders can be used in many ways besides vertically; for example, place them horizontally on the floor, or use more than one. It depends on your imagination. I once used a ladder for a satiric work entitled "Angelica". The top surface was heaven, where lying on my stomach I did a flying sequence. Then, because there was a need to return to earth for some unfinished business I descended the ladder in dance phrases and, being back on earth, accomplished my mission. Once done, I blithely returned up the ladder to heaven.

Summary:

I believe that since space is our basic necessity we should treasure it. If levels are used on stage they should be there for a purpose, crucial for the production, necessary for the performer. To see a stage cluttered with objects that are there because of a designer's whim is unjust to the performer. The precious space is whittled down and the performer is forced to work in whatever space remains. There is always the thought "I must avoid that object."

HAND PROPS

In working with hand props I advise that you find whatever is available and follow the method pattern: (1) experiment with the specific mechanics; (2) try improvs just for design (each prop with its own shape offers new ideas); (3) let imagination take over and do improvs using the prop as a symbol or association.

The sequence in the study of hand props is optional.

1 - Fans

Learning to use a fan's many possibilities is an interesting adventure. Fans come in all types and sizes from the stiff fans of the Japanese to the silk or lace of the Spanish, from huge feather fans to tiny lace confections. Each serves a particular purpose. In many cultures the fan plays an important role both in daily and in artistic life. In Japanese classical dance and theatre, besides embellishing the design of a movement, it is even more important when used metaphorically. It has a language all its own. It can be a dagger, a sword, a cane, an umbrella, a wheel, a cup (half open), a saucer (fully opened), a sake bottle, a shoji screen. a falling leaf, the wind, a letter, and two fans may be a butterfly. It may be anything you can imagine. The audience conversant with this special language has no trouble understanding what is meant. In Spanish court life the fan was used by women as a secret language. The manner in which a fan was opened or closed could send a signal to a lover where they might meet.

The fan, aside from its functions of decoration, flirtation, and keeping cool, offers a wealth of opportunity for symbolism. It can be speech emanating from the mouth by holding the low end at the mouth while opening and shutting it with a speech rhythm. It can be a heartbeat or a moon rising. I remember a study in which four girls used fans for a game of cards, and another in which the fan was first an Elizabethan collar, setting the period, and then the device for beheading Mary Queen of Scots.

A fan also has interesting dynamics. It can be opened slowly, quickly, vigorously, or delicately. There is also great variation in the sound it can make, according to the energy used in snapping it open and closed or tapping with it. Lastly much depends on the size, materials, and character of the fan.

Method

To experiment it is most practical to use simple Japanese paper fans since they are expendable.

Rhythm: 1 2

Holding the base in the palm of the R hand with thumb and

forefinger grasping the first spoke, rotate the wrist sharply down in front of body with medium energy 1 this flips open the fan. Rotate the wrist back to the R 2 which will close the fan.

Comment:

There is a very slight elbow action as wrist rotates. When you flip open you must release all the fingers except those holding the first spoke. At first the fan may not open completely (especially the paper fans which may be stiff). Fans also tend to drop out of the hand if not held firmly. This exercise should be repeated until you get the feel of opening and closing the fan with a snap. On repeating with left hand the thumb and fore finger may have to hold the fan by the last spoke in order to keep the design facing front. With good Japanese fans the design is on both sides.

Rhythm: 1 2 3 4

Hold fan open in front of chest with R hand, thumb in front, and fingers supporting the back of fan.

Rotate wrist to R extending arm directly forward 1 2 3 hold 4. Return with a reverse twist to chest on same counts.

Repeat four times forward/back.

Repeat four times to right side.

Allow four counts to change hands and repeat with left hand. Be sure not to grip too tightly. The fan must be held firmly but loosely enough to allow the fingers to adjust in the forward and back moves.

Repeat same action but add a vertical flutter on count 4

Rhythm: 1 2 3 4 5 6 7 8.

Holding fan open in R hand rotate wrist L and R (figure eight) Rising 1 - 8

Lowering 1 - 8

Repeat to R side.

Do a complete circle from L to R two counts of eight.

Repeat entire phrase on opposite side.

Repeat exercise with a space range concept from small to great while going up, great to small going down. As the movement increases the entire body becomes involved. Reverse space range, starting from great to small while going up, small to great going down. Each variation produces a completely different impact.

Rhythm: 1 2 3 4

To a count of four alternate the figure eight overhead and on a low plane. Both sides.

Rhythm: 1 2 3 4 5 6 7 8

Hold both ends of fan open in front of chest between index and third fingers, roll fan forward and down 1 2 3 4.

Toward body back and up 5 6 7 8.

Comment:

The fingers, especially the thumb, index, and third finger, must adjust by replacing each other rolling down and up. This exercise helps the dexterity of the fingers and should be repeated until the action is absolutely smooth.

Rhythm: 1 2 3 4 5 / 1 2 3 4 5

Standing profile in parallel fourth position, L leg forward, hold open fan at both ends between thumb and index fingers with R hand forward, roll fan down like a wheel toward forward leg, with body bending forward 1 2 3 4 5.

Roll back up, shifting weight to back leg 1 2 3 4 5

Constant manipulation of the fingers is required to keep the fan's original shape. Both sides.

Comment:

By using the fan and exploring various possibilities you will find that your body is forced to take on many new shapes.

Explore opening and closing the fan in an unconventional manner: using the ear, nose, elbows, toes, any part of the body. You will be amazed to discover how many new and unusual movements this process will reveal.

Do not forget that fans can be used solely for design. They shape the space, adding a new dimension. It is spellbinding to watch a group improv on design. The mere fact of the fan unifies the group no matter how diverse the movement, whereas without the fans the same improv can be fragmented and without impact. This is true when the same prop is used by everyone. The prop becomes a focal point, offering a thread that binds the group into a cohesive unit.

Singly, create an improv on design and then repeat it without the fan. The result may be that, because of the fan, the body takes on various shapes that are refreshingly different.

Explore the use of the fan as a symbol. Solo improvs are always surprising because of the uniqueness of each individual.

Comment:

In working with a fan as a symbol, the motivation of the gesture and the rhythms are major and the design is minor. On the other hand, if the motivation is design, the shape and texture are dominant. You may never have the need to use a fan but in learning to handle it a facility is acquired that can be adapted to the use of any prop.

2 - <u>Hoops</u>

Method

Rhythm: 1 2 3

Holding hoop in one hand, swing it up and around to the R 1 2 3. Four times.

Allow 1 2 3 to change hands

Repeat to the L.

Swing hoop around and let it rotate in the fingers 1 2 3.

Spin hoop on floor. Set optional rhythm.

Try rhythm ideas by beating hoop on floor.

Invent new ways of handling hoop.

Improvs for design, singly and in multiple units.

Improv using hoop as a symbol. A hoop can be a safe place for protection. It can be a prison, a pool, part of the body that you cannot escape, a mirror. It is whatever you want it to be; viewers may decide for themselves what the image is.

<u>Comment</u>:

The hoop because of its weight and shape, makes the body move differently. This creates surprising and unexpected movement. The hoop must become an integral part of the movement and not a tricky mechanical display of dexterity.

If hoops are not available I discovered and made a possible substitute that lent itself to infinitely more interesting shapes as well as sounds. Get a length of whaleboning (a strip of special tape used for stiffening costumes). Make a hoop of about fifteen-inch diameter by overlapping the tape three times. Bind the three layers with a strong binding tape in four places so that the shape of a hoop results. You will find that it has great elasticity; it can be stretched or compressed into various shapes.

Rhythm: 1 2 3

Repeat above exercises with substitute hoop.

With both hands hold the hoop in the middle and pull horizontally in opposite directions out 1 2 in 3 4. Repeat four times.

Repeat the same vertically.

Hold hoop in R hand and rebound forward 1 2 sideways 3 4 repeat four times. Change hands 1 2

Repeat with L hand.

Shake hoop for sound. Various directions and shapes produce different sounds.

Improv for design, exploring many of the possible shapes.

Improvs exploring possible symbols. It may be an arrow, a binding emotion, or physical force, a link to another person.

Group improv for design.

Group improv with a dramatic motivation.

Comment:

One group improv I witnessed started as a chain gang and included many small unit encounters that covered various emotional situations. Besides the variety of shapes and sound, this particular prop is a chameleon for innumerable metaphors. It can become almost anything you want.

3 - Chinese Ribbons

Staple two yards of ribbon one-and-a-half or two inches wide to a twelve-or fourteen-inch dowel. This is a prop commonly used in Chinese dance. If the proper energy is not used the ribbon may become knotted, wrap itself about the body, or simply wilt to the floor. Once the technique of handling is mastered, the ribbons become a fascinating challenge for shaping new dimensions in space as well as body movement. When this is converted to symbolic use, the idea plus the visual factor create an unusual effect. These ribbons though Chinese in origin have been used with great effect in many works both decoratively and with motivation.

Method

Rhythm: 1 2 3 4 (slow)

Facing front, holding stick in R hand at arm's length do four large circles outside, front of body, 1 2 3 4

Reverse direction allowing the wrist to make a small scoop, and do four inside circles, 1 2 3 4.

Repeat with left hand.

Comment:

The initial attack of the circle should have maximum energy. It is the amount of energy used that will keep the ribbon from twisting into knots or brushing the floor. The total body should participate in the movement.

Rhythm: 1 2 3

Start the single outside circle 1

Add an overhead circle 2

Finish original circle 3

Reverse to inside circle and repeat on opposite side.

Rhythm: 1& 2&

Describe a horizontal figure eight swing R hand up to left 1

down &

Up to R 2

Down toward left &.

The up movement has greater energy, the down has less

energy. Reverse the dynamics so that the down has the greater energy, the up less.

Changing the dynamics has an entirely different effect both emotionally and physically.

Rhythm: 1 2 3

One large circle to the R 1

Finish with a horizontal ripple to R 2 3.

Repeat four times to R and four times to the L.

Comment:

The ripple is achieved by a fast up-and-down move of the wrist. The vertical space range

of the wrist determines the size of the ripple.

Rhythm:1 2 3

Sweep ribbon up front of body 1

Ripple down 2 3.

R arm four times

L arm four times.

Use free hand to create tensions of the ribbon by pulling it taut.

Experiment to find designs not related to space but to the body, Try any move, including

a turn with use of the ribbon.

Try a fall without getting so entangled in the ribbon that recovery is impossible. It is

wise to try the fall without the ribbon, then find a way of embellishing the fall by use of

the ribbon.

Try various leaps and jumps using ribbon in all possible ways.

Comment:

Ribbons can symbolize a weapon, a noose, a flag, a lariat. They can become a restriction by winding around the body. They also make sound, depending on the initial energy used. The dynamics of the sound can be used rhythmically, dramatically, or for punctuation.

Improv singly for design.

Improv with several people for design. In this improv, space is most important. You must be spaced enough apart to avoid entanglement, but if it does happen you have the challenge of inventing movement to free yourselves. This could very easily happen on a small stage. Always be aware that the unexpected is a possibility in any performance.

Improv singly using ribbon as symbol, for example wrapping and unwinding yourself in personal discovery, or the reverse: be free and then get entangled as though trapped by your own personality.

Group improv using ribbons symbolically. There are myriad ideas such as breaking the group into smaller units until a unified force brings them together, or beginning with a unified idea which fragments until all are isolated.

Comment:

Ribbons can be any width - even as wide as flags - any length, any texture. The sticks may be any length, depending on the specific motivation. The color and particularly the texture dictate how they should be handled. Using a metallic ribbon, one student wound it tightly. Then, holding the stick vertically with the rolled ribbon facing down, the most amazing effect resulted: the ribbon spiralled down vertically like water falling and resembled an icicle or a shining tube. I then had a group of five stand in a semicircle, allowing their ribbons to unroll at their own timing. It became a waterfall and then changed, looking like aluminum tubes. I had them walk where they wished, passing or around each other. The effect was magical as it took on the aspect of a strange ritual. The texture must be of very fine metallic ribbon. The imagination of one very talented student helped discover an entirely new way for using the ribbon.

4 - Chairs

Manipulations with a chair can generate a wealth of symbolic ideas:

Tipped on its side with the back facing front, it can become a gate.

If you lie on the floor behind an upright chair and creep under it, it becomes a cage.

Tilt it with back of chair on the floor and it may be a couch.

Strap it to your back and it becomes a burden.

It can be a place of security, a refuge.

Comment:

There are so many possibilities it is impossible to mention them all. Through imagination, each of you will discover the total potential of such a simple prop, and its availability makes it easy to explore.

5 - Umbrellas

Umbrellas can be explored in the same way as chairs. They may be used for design or symbolically. The potential is endless.

6 - Elastic

Elastic is a wonderful prop because of its versatility: it stretches, shrinks, can be twisted into any shape. Besides the variety of design, the symbolism that it can evoke is infinite. Make a loop of elastic two inches wide and about twenty-seven inches long by joining the ends of a fifty-four inch length. You now have a prop that will challenge the imagination. You can open the space to the outside world or be enclosed by it, you can be bound or linked to someone else. You can grow tall, or small; use it as a whip, a lariat, a support, speech, a heartbeat, an umbilical cord, or a life line. The elastic can become whatever you wish.

Method

Placing the hands in opposite ends of the loop, open the arms to both sides horizontally.

With hands in same position, stretch the elastic vertically.

Place foot on floor in loop; with R hand push loop up.

Foot in same position, push loop up with both hands apart.

Try various shapes with foot off floor; with body tilts.

Investigate various shapes and possibilities with elastic.
Improv singly, then with group for design.

Symbolic improv singly, then in group or any unit more than one.

Comment:

Elastic does not necessarily have to be a loop or any specific width depending on the motivation and personal preference. It can be a single length of any dimension from very short to the length of the entire stage.

After exploring all possibilities of a particular prop, I tend to use it symbolically. In a work called "The Farewell" (a tribute to Doris Humphrey) a white rope ringing the stage in a semicircle is the memory line; a white elastic band - two inches wide, cutting diagonally across the stage, and anchored to the floor - is the life line. The program note:

"Our shimmering memories we take with us
The luminous self we leave to others"

After each of the first three sections (which are flashbacks), "To The Earth" "To Youth" "To Love", I gather a section of the rope, and exit after the third with the entire rope. The final section "The Last Farewell" deals with the elastic which symbolizes tears, a burden, and I am caught in its meshes. At the end, while two people hidden in the wings slowly raise the elastic, I exit holding the elastic high and let it snap back as I clear the wing.

THE LUMINOUS SELF WE LEAVE TO OTHERS.

FABRIC

A knowledge of cloth, with its various textures and weights is important from the standpoint of use as a prop as well as for costumes. Working with various lengths from small pieces to lengths that fill the stage is a challenge. The weight of a piece of fabric determines the amount of energy needed to handle it. China silk or chiffon need very little energy; they seem to float in the air. Velvet, which is heavy, needs strong energy to make it move or catch the air. Pure silk or pure velvet will move quite differently from their synthetic substitutes. Cotton does not float as easily as rayon. Therefore you must learn to adapt to the idiosyncrasies. Try to collect all kinds of cloth - a variety of lengths, shapes, and textures - with which to experiment. If you work with an institution that has a costume department ask for leftover pieces. If not, do not throw away anything that might be of use. Keep a scrapbox of odds and ends.

1 - Design
Method

Start with a light-weight fabric. If several people are working simultaneously, always allow adequate space for the use of the fabric.

Rhythm: 1 2

Hold cloth at an edge with the R hand and swing it up to the R so that it catches air and billows up 1

Down 2

Repeat four times.

Change to L hand.

Repeat same four times.

Comment:

The first thing you discover is that using your arms with varying dynamics makes the cloth respond differently. If you swing up and just pull down it will do one thing, while if you swing under on the down it will curve.

Swing up and curve under on the down move. The length and texture of the particular piece you work with will condition the muscle intensity and the energy used to achieve the desired effect.

Rhythm: 1& 2&

Holding the fabric with arms spread apart, billow it upon 1&.

On down movement circle arms bringing them together 2&.

Comment:

This changes the shape of the cloth for it will catch the air and balloon out as the arms come in. This may be done in any possible direction. The shape can be changed by the way the arms are used. Changing the energy on certain beats produces not only varying shapes but also sounds.

Rhythm: 1 2 3

Holding the fabric at one end with R hand describe a circle to R in front of body. If cloth is too long, bunch a section in the L hand allowing what is needed in the R hand.

Repeat six times changing the energy every two circles

Two circles on 1 two circles on 2 two circles on 3.

Repeat on left side

Comment:

By changing the energy, a sense of dynamics is introduced, which increases interest and changes the emotional impact. Always remember that the whole body is involved in any movement you make. (When working with a group divide the group into three sections.

First group accent 1, second 2, and third 3. A very interesting phrase results within one bar of music.)

Rhythm: 1 2

Holding cloth at one end with R hand, billow up front 1.

Whip down with a sharp accent 2.

Repeat four times alternating front and side.

Repeat opposite side.

Comment: The whipping creates a sharp sound that will vary with the texture of the fabric. Use the variety of sound as well as the visual effects.

(With a group, divide into two units. One unit starts front, the second starts side. There are many combinations of rhythms when working with more than one person so that one should be free to create.)

Comment:

If the pieces of cloth have different weights, interchange them so that you learn how much energy is needed to handle each weight.

Rhythm: 1 2 3

Holding cloth by one end swing to R 1

Circle L overhead 2

Come down to L 3.

Repeat four times both sides.

Rhythm: 1 2 3 4 5 6 7 8

Bunching up cloth in L hand, leaving about one-half yard or so hanging in R hand, spiral up (rotate wrist L to R) 1 - 8

Spiral down (rotate wrist L to R) 1 - 8. Repeat four times. Allow four counts to change hands and repeat with L hand.

Change dynamics. Starting with R hand small space range and increasing space range on up spiral 1 - 8

Diminish on down spiral 1 - 8

Repeat with left hand. Body should sway with the spiral, the texture determining the sway.

Comment:

for the small space range, the arm moves from elbow. As the range grows the entire arm becomes involved.

Bunch cloth in both hands, allowing hanging ends. Repeat above with two hands.

Rhythm: 1 2 3

Holding cloth at edge with both hands spread apart and facing front, circle to L overhead allowing R hand to cross over L hand. Continue circle by following with L hand overhead. R hand continues circle. As right comes down L crosses over and arms open up in front of body 1 2 3

Repeat four times - reverse.

Comment:

Although this maneuver sounds complicated verbally, it actually flows very easily. It introduces a swirling twist, which is used by matadors when working with a circular cape in the bull ring. The crossing of one hand over the other can be used in various ways and directions.

Moving in space using the fabric only for design can be very exciting. The body as well as the space becomes part of the movement of the cloth.

Holding one end, swing and turn, scoop under, leap, invent ways of using the various fabrics for design.

Improvs based on design singly and in small groups open a new area for investigation.

Rhythm: 1 2

Holding fabric bunched in the R hand, pull it toward the body with the L hand 1 2

Repeat four times. The effect is of anger.

Change hands and direction bunching fabric with L hand, pull it away from body with the R hand 1 2. The effect is of ridding oneself of something. Add more body movement and the emotional feel becomes stronger.

Spiral it up and down very fast, creating a sharp sound.

Billow it slowly in a spiral, producing a gentle sound. The sound of the cloth can be effective in silence as well as with music.

Rebound the hand or arm; the fabric also rebounds. This is useful for emphasis.

2 - Symbol

Fabric of different textures and weights is a wonderful device for symbolic use. It can take on almost any symbol or association you wish. The sound adds to the potential. It is the amount of muscle intensity and the timing that create the difference. It can be a burden, a child, the wind, a weapon, a robe, a piece of clothing, a private territory, fate, an enemy, a rope, a magic force. It can also serve as an association that triggers a specific memory. There is no limit except the power of each individual's invention, imagination, and creativity.

Method

Solo improv, with personal choice of a type of fabric.

Improv with a texture that is different from the first

Improvs in groups of two, three, or as many as desired.

3 - <u>Long Fabric</u>

Using a length of ten to fifteen yards reaps very unusual images. It may be straight cloth, but if it is stretch material it is even more exciting. Experiment to find the feel of the fabric. The long fabric offers a chance for limitless discovery. Allow time for fiddling with it singly and in units from three to four people. It is spellbinding to see the unusual shapes and ideas that emerge. Many are accidental and should be recalled.

Method

Solo improv aiming for whatever design can be achieved with such a long piece. You soon discover that the sculptural images trigger the imagination. When working alone you are free to do anything you wish: the entire length is there to be used, from wrapping yourself in it to flinging it in all directions.

Improv for design with more than one person. When working with others, be very aware of what they are doing and relate to them, since the one length binds the people and the movement potential.

Solo improv using fabric as a symbol. Seek a motivation: a web in which you are caught or a burden of which you try to rid yourself. At times it overpowers you. Eventually you may discover it is not really a burden at all, but hope. Be aware of the tensions that can be achieved with this fabric and how it may constantly change. Fabric has the faculty of becoming part of our body more than other props. This can be a danger. It is easy to become so infatuated with the shapes that the original idea is lost.

   In a solo work, "Cassandra" I used an eighteen-yard length of heavy black crepe, held on the floor by an assistant in the downstage right wing. It was draped along the side of the stage to be hung from an overhead batten directly behind two platforms. This gave the impression of the entrance to a temple. In the final section of the dance, called "Frenzy" I jumped on the platform and ripped the fabric down over my head. With careful manipulation I walked downstage left and threw it into the wing, where it was caught by an attendant. The fabric held taut across the stage, became an image of doom, of fate, of tears as I worked with it. At the final moment, standing center stage, I pulled both ends violently over my head as the helpers released the ends. The whole length of fabric flew in from the wings - a black cloud of Fate enshrouding me. Besides its many symbols it also created a tremendous dramatic effect. Yet it was only a long piece of fabric.

Group improv, symbolic. Three or four people. The relationship of the group must be evident. The single length of the fabric is a unifying factor, although the motivation may involve many diverse attitudes. Let the imagination take over and as the improv develops it may take an unexpected turn that will surprise both participants and viewers alike.

Tubular Stretch Cloth

This type of cloth can take on strange sculptural shapes if you are in the tube. It can elongate, stretch in width or shrink. Tubular two-way stretch cloth has infinite possibilities.

Martha Graham's "Lamentation" is an excellent example of how the tensions of a tube of stretch cloth create a tremendous emotional impact. Just by sitting on a small bench encased in the tube, she made the shapes and tension become the very essence of grief. However this is not achieved by the sheer manipulation of the cloth. It stems from a deep emotional motivation that uses the cloth as a medium for that emotion.

Comment:

Tensions can be achieved by the use of hands, feet, any part of the body, or between two or more people. You must be certain that these tensions serve a purpose either for design or for other motivation.

4 - Association

Improvs using fabric as an association. The fabric is not a symbol; it remains simply what it is but triggers a memory or a thought that develops emotionally.

Comment:

It is very important never to reveal the mechanics; otherwise all illusion is lost. Learn how to manipulate the fingers, to keep fabric from slipping. With slippery fabric be aware of traction. If you step on it you may fall and be injured. Always make certain what the feet are doing in relation to the cloth. If you swing or whip it know how much energy to use to keep it clear of your legs. Always be sure it will not hit someone.

Do not allow yourself to be so carried away by the prop that it becomes an improv of prop with dancer rather than the reverse. Another warning; allow time for the shapes and images to have an impact. Sometimes we are so fascinated with manipulation that the sculptural and emotional impact is lost.

COSTUME

A choreographer often has in mind a costume that will have a long skirt. However, all through the rehearsal period the performer works in tights. Then just before performance, the costume arrives with an ankle-length skirt. Sometimes panic sets in. The choreographer is in for a shock. Besides the problems of working in the skirt on short notice, the movement looks wrong. Why? Movement that may feature complicated leg combinations is completely hidden by the skirt. The lack of familiarity with handling the skirt adds to the difficulty.

If the performer is to be costumed other than in tights, a mock costume of some cheap fabric should be made at the outset of rehearsals. The choreographic lines will be different. It may not be a skirt, but a caftan, puffed sleeves, padded knickers for a man's period costume, a toga, or some sort of drapery, which could change the original concept of the movement or demand specific handling. If a long circular skirt is involved, the skirt itself suggests new possibilities for invention, not only for movement but also for shaping the space itself. The creative images that skirts offer provide a new area in the search for fresh and original movement. There are many styles of long skirts, but for practical purposes I recommend working with a floor-length skirt that is at least one circle or more wide. Experimenting with the mechanics puts you at ease, so that you can concentrate on the quality of performance rather than the fear of stepping on the skirt, tripping, or getting hopelessly wound up in a fall.

The mechanics of skirt handling often relies on the dynamics. The energy with which you raise your leg will cause the skirt to react in various ways, depending on the texture: the same amount of energy may make a velvet skirt look heavy and dignified and one of chiffon billowy or frothy. If at all possible, it is advisable to have skirts of various weights.

1 -Skirts

Long Skirts: Leg Moves

Method

Rhythm: 1 2 3 4 5 6 7 8

In a plié so that skirt drags on floor, walk forward 1 - 8

Walk back 1 - 8.

It will be almost impossible to avoid stepping on the skirt.

Walk forward, sliding the foot along the floor and pushing the edge of the skirt forward 1 - 8

Walk back in the same way 1 - 8

This safeguards against stepping on the skirt.

Travel to the right crossing one foot over the other 1 - 8

Travel to the left crossing one foot over the other 1 - 8

Imagine there is a twelve-inch added length to the back of the skirt (as I had in "The Moor's Pavane"). Moving back, you must look at ease and yet be sure to conceal the handling of the skirt. With the arm close to the body lift the skirt in back so that the foot is clear of the skirt. In tucking the skirt up in back, it is the wrist rather than the elbow that raises it up. Hide the arm completely, making certain to keep the focus of the viewer on you by some small gesture with the free arm. Walk forward on 8 and back on 8 without attracting attention to the arm maneuver.

Repeat, but this time use both hands.

The difference is that, with both hands, the gesture of picking up the skirt must be made as an obvious dance move.

The focus must be concentrated on the gesture.

Dynamics, especially the time element and the muscle intensity, play a large role in achieving certain effects. If the knee is pulled up sharply, with great energy, the skirt will flip. On the other hand, if little energy is used the skirt will rest on the leg or swing lyrically. In Spanish dance this use of the skirt is vital to the core of the movement.

Rhythm: 1& 2&

Facing front, sharply raise and lower R knee bent, forward 1&

Repeat with L knee 2&

Repeat knee to each side

To make the skirt flip in back, the lower part of the leg is used with a bend of the knee; the foot creates the flip. This is effective in turns.

For the skirt to move smoothly, less energy is needed. This allows the skirt to rest on the leg. The skirt will take on any shape of the leg, but will extend the leg move by continuing to move in time and space even after the leg move itself has stopped.

For a large circular sweep, elongate the leg to a wide arc; with a rond de jambe of any kind the skirt will create wonderful shapes.

Rhythm: Legato 1 2 3/ 1 2/ 1

Turn left with an inside rond de jambe of the R leg. The skirt will circle in a large scoop.

Legato 1 2 3

Repeat 1 2

Repeat 1

Comment:

The dynamic change in timing changes the shape and the intensity of the skirt movement. The change of intensity creates an entirely different emotional quality

Holding Skirt

There are many ways of holding a skirt. There are definite period styles, ethnic styles, and finally sheer functional needs relative to the movement. The wrists often play a strong role. The point is never to allow yourself to get caught in the skirt.

Method

Rhythm: 1 2&

Travelling in a circle with small back pas de chat jump R 1

land L 2 step R &. This step alternates.

To clear the legs in front, hold the skirt with two hands, just high enough to clear the feet, elbows out, wrists turned in. This lends a period look. The same step done holding the skirt at the sides with long arms will change the look.

Holding the skirt with one hand at arm's length while doing a waltz step immediately associates the look with the Viennese waltz. Try various phrases of movement to discover all the functional and decorative ways of handling the skirt.

3 - <u>Skirt and Levels</u>

When you work with steps and levels in a long costume you have to discover ways of clearing the feet while going up or down and still look comfortable and secure. Lift the skirt, without groping, before going up or down the steps. Make the lifting an important gesture - a planned gesture.

Wearing the skirt try some of the phrases on levels (see stage props). Many problems will be encountered and solving them may be of help in the future.

Solo improv on various levels in the skirts, including turning, and leaping.

Group improvs with three people: be aware of the spacing.

<u>Skirts: Design</u>

Skirts can be can designed with infinite variety. Each type will demand a different means of handling in order to alter the shape of space design. There are short skirts that are controlled by body movement. Long skirts that cling in front but with fishtail fullness in back move in a completely different way and depend more on dynamics and the hand. There are skirts with slits on the side or in front and wrap-around skirts. Each demands a knowledge of specialized mechanics.

Method

Rhythm: 1 2 3 4 5 6 7 8

Holding an end, spiral up, using wrist as with fan 1 - 8

Spiral down 1 - 8

Repeat changing space range, small to great up, to small down. Repeat again, reversing space range, great to small to great.

Allow four counts to change hands and repeat all three phrases.

Falls with skirts present a problem. Both in the fall and the recovery a way must be found of clearing the feet and the body so that they are free to move. If you land on a part of the skirt there must be instantaneous invention to find a deliberate movement for clearing the skirt that will look like part of the recovery. Never reveal by fumbling that there is trouble; it marks the difference between the amateur and the professional. Falls must be rehearsed in the skirt many times, for the same thing rarely happens twice. The moment you feel a pull of the fabric release the limb or that area of the body, allowing the cloth to give.

Do a fall and recovery singly.

Repeat same in groups of two or three.

Improvs for design, with two or three people   Remove the skirts and try to repeat the improv. The contrast is apparent; it becomes dull. The tendency always to work in tights is necessary for technique but for creative movement both are helpful.

Skirts: Symbolic

Skirts have an enormous range of symbolic use. They can express many kinds of emotions and objects.

Joy: holding an edge, flutter the skirt with an inner focus of joy. The flutter may indicate laughter.

Fear: Holding an edge flutter the skirt with an inner focus of fear. The flutter will indicate a quickening heartbeat.

Anger, frustration, anxiety: hold an edge in one hand, rip edge through the fingers of other hand.

A weapon: bunch a portion in one hand and whip it sharply.

A burden: carry a part of it or drape it over the shoulder with the sense of weight.

A child: hold a portion in the arms and rock it.

Tears: holding two ends and standing in low attitude, alternate hands, bringing skirt close to eyes. May indicate tears falling.

A binding force: wrap yourself in the skirt - unable to get free.

Create a solo improv, using skirt as a symbol.
Create improvs with two or more people using skirt as a symbol.

Comment:

Besides using the skirt as a skirt, there are interesting ways to change the skirt into another kind of costume: worn around the neck it becomes a cape or a jerkin; worn over one shoulder with the other arm free it becomes a toga; worn across the chest it can be a child's dress; with the front of the waistline draped under the chin and the back of skirt pulled over the face, it becomes a screening device, a veil, or a symbol of blindness. In Limón's "There Is a Time" a slit skirt was draped in various ways. In my "Out of This Sorrow" I used two skirts, one of them draped overhead like a shawl. When I dropped it dramatically, it became a Spanish costume.

2 - Caftans

A caftan, because of its versatility, is an endless source for imaginative design and symbolism. Basically, it is very simple to make. Measure the length from neck to toe.

Use a piece of cloth double the length, fold in half, and slit an opening for the head at the center of the fold. Voila! A caftan. Now the imagination should take over by sewing a series of very large hooks and eyes in strategic places. I have put a hook and eye at the waist of the front panel. There are also snaps at the four corners of the caftan and matching eyes, two in front and two in back, at the far edges of the neck opening. It offers a multiple use for shaping the caftan at will.

As a suggestion, this is how I used caftans for a piece entitled "Cantigas" which deals with medieval and contemporary times. I lined them in two colors - one side in peacock blue and the other side in black; the outer side was in various shades of yellow gold. I was able to use the caftans in multiple ways for visual interest and exciting dramatic effects.

Fastening the waistline hook and eye of the front panel in back of the body defined the front of the body while the back lined in the blue hung loose. This, with the outer sides in tones of gold, was used for one of the medieval sections.

Fastening the lower corners to the neckline gave very beautiful tunics of different colors (the two colors of the lining showing on the gold).

With all the bodies (in unitards) lying on the floor, the caftans were spread over them so that when they rose, the black was toward the audience. The dancers walked upstage, blending into a black backdrop, turned slowly to walk downstage revealing the blue, and finally twirled in place as they reversed the caftans and the entire stage turned gold.

Holding a back corner raised back with outstretched hand diagonally up, they turned the caftans into banners. This was motivated by a dramatic idea and had a breathtaking theatrical effect on the audience.

Comment:

You should feel free to do whatever you please with a specific length of cloth. It need not be a caftan. It can be draped as a toga or drawn through the legs. It can be almost anything.

3 - <u>Style</u>

Adapting movement to costume - period, ethnic, or modern - is an area that requires a book of its own. I prefer not to explore it except for a few suggestions. Many times a work is done that implies a period style, but the costume and the movement are not authentic. All that is desired is the flavor of the period. It might be Elizabethan, but only a stiff collar framing the head is used as a costume device. Head movement will be restricted, thus suggesting a sense of the style. If large puffed sleeves or other costume devices are used the arms will be kept a certain distance from the body. A portrait of an Infanta in the time of Velasquez certainly proves that extended side panniers do not permit the   arms to hang straight down at the sides; they will have to be held out from the body. So, even if the costume and movement are not very authentic, a small detail in the movement can create a sense of a period.

Various types of shoes also contribute to style. If a work demands a certain type of shoe, it is important to wear some kind of shoe from the very first rehearsal. Modern dancers accustomed to working barefoot may have to learn to work in ballet shoes. Performers may be required to wear shoes with low or high heels, or boots. Each of these require adjustment in traction, balance, and dynamics. The performer should be given the chance to adapt as soon as possible.

PART 5 - STAGE DECORUM
BOWS

1 - Definition

Bows are tremendously important to the performer. It is the final view the audience has of you as performer. What does a bow really mean? It means, "I thank you for your attention. I thank you for your appreciation. I thank you for your graciousness." A bow should never be an egoistic "I deserve this bow, I know I was great."

There should be dignity, poise, and graciousness, coupled with sincerity. You must care that the audience calls you back to thank you. Group bows should be planned and rehearsed. There is nothing as amateurish as a group of people taking a bow at variance with each other; it embarrasses the audience as well as the performers.

Very often a bow can reveal the true personality of the performer: arrogant, humble, embarrassed, or shy. Train yourself to be honest, and retain the integrity of the performance through the very final bow.

There are many ways of taking bows

Blackout or curtain - quickly take the place desired for the bow lights up and bow, blackout or curtain.

Same as above, but exit in the light (blackouts save time).

Blackout or curtain - clear fast - lights up - enter from wing, bow, exit - blackout or curtain.

Blackout or curtain - group of performers of equal importance; enter from the wing, cross the front of the stage in quick succession with small bow, exit. This can be effective.

Blackout or curtain - ensemble takes assigned places - lights up, bow - feed remainder of cast in order, with soloists entering last blackout - lights up with cast in place for follow-up bows.

I am certain that there are many more possibilities than these.

Make sure that bow lights are set in the cue sheet.

When taking a bow do not dash out, bob down quickly, and leave. At the moment of a bow it is advisable to take a breath, focus directly at audience, and bow. Say to yourself, "I thank you." Not only say it, but honestly feel it. This allows the proper time for acknowledging the applause. An important element is to look comfortable. Find a way of using the body and the arms that seems right for you.

I find it advantageous to vary the bows for different pieces, considering the nature of the particular work. After a serious piece it would be silly to prance out gaily. With a light piece a somber mien would be just as silly. After a comic work taking a funny bow can become kitsch. It sometimes feels like the piece is starting over again, unless very carefully handled.

Comment:

For solo women's bows it may feel correct to cross one foot behind and bend the body, placing the hands where comfortable. In a period costume the skirt might be held in one hand or both hands. Some prefer to extend one or both arms on the curtsy. Ballet dancers usually take their solo bows with a deep bend in the knees, head bent down, and arms extended. This seems to be the traditional ballerina bow. In modern dance the bow has no particular tradition.

Men should keep feet together, take a breath, and bend at the waist, with an arm either extended or crossed at the waist, or allow both arms to hang comfortably at the side of the body.

There is a certain acknowledged ritual in the order of group bows, starting with the company dancers, followed by the soloists according to their importance, and finally those who perform the leading parts. There is a valid reason for this order: it keeps the applause alive, for the audience will continue to applaud until the most important performers take their bow. It is up to the choreographer to set the bows and to keep them interesting: different shapes on stage, various entrances from wings, crossing the stage individually, and so forth.

A sense of proper timing is absolutely essential. Nothing is as embarrassing as being caught on stage when the applause has stopped. You must listen to the volume of the applause; this demands hypersensitive hearing and instant decision.

2 - Timing

Method:

Enter singly, bow, exit. Unless you are experienced, this usually is a fiasco as well as a comedy: too fast, too slow, too awkward, or too self-conscious.

Rhythm: 1 2 3 4

Girls: take a breath and step R 1 2

Bring L foot back of R and bend with small plié 3 4.

Repeat four times, alternating sides

This can apply for solo or group bows if there are only girls.

Men: follow above phrase and keeping feet together (do not cross feet). In solo bows you may hold one arm extended or across waist and bend body. In group bows, it seems better to let the arms hang naturally at the sides.

3 - Solo

The remainder of the group should represent the audience applauding. In this way it is easier to practice timing.

Loud applause; enter at a medium pace, bow, exit slightly faster.

Medium applause: enter quicker pace, bow, exit at a slow run.

Light applause; run on without looking rushed, bow slightly faster, run off.

If doubtful of applause, take bow close to wing and exit.

Comment:

For all exits be certain to clear the wings. Do not be caught on stage when lights come up after blackout. If the applause sounds as if it is dying, it is best not to come out because the applause may not last long enough.

4 - Duet

The man leads on stage, hand across body holding woman's hand. As he travels, he allows her to pass in front of him. Both face audience, take a breath, bow. Exit; same side, man again leads woman, allows her to pass him, and woman exits first, or exit opposite sides.

Enter same way, bow, the man steps back while the woman takes a solo bow, the man comes forward and they exit as above.

Enter same, bow center stage, both dancers two steps back, face each other and bow, exit.

Enter from opposite sides, meet at center, bow, to audience, step back and bow to each other, exit together or to respective entrances.

Comment:

For more than two performers the choreographer should set a particular pattern for the entrances and exits.

5 - Group

Blackout or curtain: the performers take their places on stage, lights or curtain up.

Have two rows in staggered spacing. The women in the front row the men behind.

The women in the front row bow.

The rows interchange three steps.

The men in front row bow.

They form a single line and bow together.

For succeeding bows it can be a straight line with special dancers stepping forward singly and then a unison bow.

Blackout or curtain: first bow straight line, dancers holding hands, step forward one or two steps, raise arms and bow in unison.

Second bow keep same line, soloist enters, bows, front of line, joins line, in center, all hold hands up and unison bow.

Various shapes possible: semi-circles, triangles, diagonals, through which the soloists can make special entrances.

Comment:

For group bows assign a person, most visible to the group, who can cue the moves. This avoids confusion and lends a professional look to the bows.

Designate a performer to motion or to lead the choreographer to come on stage for a bow. The choreographer should bow to the audience and then acknowledge those on stage.

If live music is used, the soloist should acknowledge the conductor, by a gesture to him in the pit. If he has time to come onstage, he should join the company for a bow.

Solo musicians should also be included in the final bows.

Bows are a very personal matter for the choreographer or the theater director and should be planned and rehearsed, well in advance as part of the performance at all final run-through.

ENTRANCES AND EXITS

1 - Entrances

The performer should be aware of the sightlines in the theater. Be certain you are not visible to the audience before the moment of an entrance.

It is best to stand deep in the wings, if possible.

If the wing space is shallow, stand with the back flat against the wing, that makes you less visible.

What is most vital is to maintain inner focus while still being aware of any surrounding problems. Such problems may vary from theater to theater.

Waiting in the wings for an entrance should be considered part of the performance, never a rest. Yes, you may need to catch your breath or restore your energy, but always remain in the spirit of the piece. It helps to watch what is happening on stage.

You are the performer, whether on or off stage. You must maintain your concentration from the moment the piece begins till the moment the curtain finally closes.

2 - Exits

If the costume is long or has a train, be sure that not only you but the costume are clear from view.

Be careful of the shinbusters in exits.

If you have several entrances and exits during a work, the inner focus must be constantly maintained; even when making a costume change. Otherwise, the intensity of the performance is lost because of the lack of continuity. With probable backstage noise and confusion it may be difficult to concentrate but with practice a certain discipline is acquired.

That discipline, difficult as it may be, is essential for the performer.

On making an exit, at the end of a work, never drop the inner focus until you are completely out of sight.

PART 6 - REMINDERS

If you are a member of a major company, some of these reminders may not apply. However, if you are a soloist or a member of a small company that may have to perform anywhere from a high school gym to a large theater, these reminders may help to prevent unwanted problems - including accidents.

1 - Awareness of Light

Most performers rely on the light designer to light a work, feeling that this is not the concern of the performer. But a knowledge of some simple elements of light can be of tremendous help in enhancing a performance.

There are times when a stage cannot accommodate the light plot of the designer: there is not enough equipment, or instead of lekos (spotlights that give intense light and have a hard edge) there are only fresnels (spotlights that are not sharp and have a fuzzy edge). The designer may have to compensate by altering part of the original light plot. The performer should be alert to such change. At a dress rehearsal it is important to take note of the change and adjust to it as much as possible.

If the light design includes special spotlights to highlight a particular moment, it is not enough just to be in that light; you have to be in the hotspot (that area of the spotlight which has the greatest intensity).

Some performers, not aware of the importance of movement being seen, end up in a dark area where the impact of the movement and the performance are entirely lost to the viewer. This can sometimes (unless it is inevitable) ruin an important moment in the choreography.

2 - Checking the Stage

The surface of the stage is vital to a good performance. This is as important for the dancer as a musical instrument is for a musician. Go over the stage surface before or during dress rehearsal and make mental notes.

Check the traction. Is it slippery or sticky? Is rosin needed or rubber on the soles of slippers or shoes?

Are there nails obtruding, cracks, or holes which could be dangerous?

Check the stage markers that give a sense of the stage proportion.

3 - Checking the Wings

How deep are they?

What is their masking for exits and entrances?

Where are the light booms stationed in the wings?

What clearance is there if you have to exit in a leap?

Are there weights anchoring the wings? (These are heavy oblong iron blocks; hitting one with a foot or even a toe can be very painful as well as serious).

Various stages may have a different number of wings. If there are multiple entrances and exits in quick succession from opposite sides, be sure that proper clearance is set or there could be a head on collision.

Comment:

It is very important to be extremely quiet while waiting in the wings, as a courtesy to those on stage. Any alien sound may disturb the performer's concentration and ruin an extraordinary moment for that person.

4 - Behind the Scenes

Beware of unknown obstacles which can sometimes cause a serious accident. Always be on the alert!

Be aware of the electrical wiring back stage. It is easy to trip, or inadvertently disconnect a plug.

Check where props, to be put on stage later, are placed.

For quick backstage changes, be sure to place the costumes carefully, and if necessary assign someone to help.

In a company without a wardrobe person, pick up all your personal backstage possessions; costumes, combs, brushes, makeup, leg warmers, old ballet shoes and so forth - and return them to the dressing room. Hang the costumes on hangers immediately to dry.

5 - Checking Costumes

Always look through your costumes before a performance.

Are all the hooks and eyes firmly in place?

Are any seams ripped?

Are there any rips that might have happened since the last performance?

Are the costumes properly pressed?

Check all headdresses, hair pieces, hats, hair ribbons, flowers. In other words, everything that has to do with the head. Be sure to anchor them securely.

Shoe elastics have a way of coming loose gradually. If not monitored they can snap on stage.

Pointe shoe ribbons must also be checked in good time to allow for repair.

Shoes and boots should be looked at regularly to allow for repair.

If the company has a wardrobe person, much of the above is seen to. Nevertheless a personal check may be a good idea. Run a wardrobe check between a matinee and evening performance.

6 - Checking Sound

If taped sound is used for the performance, even if the levels have been set at dress rehearsal, always have the stage manager recheck the sound before the house opens. If you do not carry personal sound equipment, but must use house facilities, sound may become a problem. Speakers blow or the volume has changed because of inaccurate volume calibrators.

CONCLUSION

The artist and craftsman ... is continually willing

his work. He devotes his life to acts which are a

personal commitment to value ... using his lifetime

to find his original face, to awaken his own voice,

beyond all learning, habit, thought: to tap life at

its source.   Centering M.C. Richards

Part of being a total artist is to seek perfection. But what is perfection? Do we really

know? To me the never-ending search for that ephemeral goal is the difference between

DOING and BEING

My goal has been to stimulate the performer to search, to discover the self hidden behind

all the learned physical technique.

Art is a human activity having for its purpose

transmission to others of the highest and best

feelings to which men have risen.

                    What is Art? Count Leo Tolstoy

The specific exercises given in this small volume are simply examples of how you may

go about experiencing the various aspects of performance. It is totally up to you to create

your own exercises or embellish the given ones. What is essential is the theory behind

the method. There is no end for serious in-depth experimentation guided by your sense

of individuality. Although the analysis demands mental recognition, the vital aspect is

to absorb it kinesthetically. It must become a body reflex, reaching your deepest feeling,

the very center of being.

103

Artistic growth is, more than anything else a

refining of the sense of truthfulness . . . Only

the artist, the great artist knows how difficult

it is.   <u>Song of the Lark</u>   Willa Cather

These quotations from three diverse writers seem to emphasize the importance of a universal truth: our deepest innermost feeling is an essential of art.

That same feeling is an essential for the performer as artist. Each time we think we have reached the seed of true feeling there is the need to dig ever deeper. As we grow more mature, our life experience teaches us more. Our emotional resources become much richer - there is more to draw upon. This growth is never-ending; thus, our understanding of art and the performing artist is constantly changing. Nuance, color, and contrast become more and more subtle. Each performance is a new experience, a new challenge. We must make greater demands of ourselves. The realm of discovery has a rare quality of mystery all its own. Each performance should be an adventure in the known and the unknown.

The details . . . he should omit and give us

only the spirit and the splendor

<u>Essay</u>: <u>Art</u> Ralph Waldo Emerson

Why struggle to be an artist?

Is it worth it?

And I answer yes, yes, and again yes.

To reach that incandescent moment of fulfillment

Is a transcending experience.

This happens rarely

It feeds the need to go on

To search and capture that moment again.

INDEX